Alexander Surname

Ireland: 1600s to 1900s

From Ireland Church Records of Baptism, Marriage and Death

Comprised of Roman Catholic and Church of Ireland Records

From Counties Carlow, Cork, Kerry and Dublin City

Compiled by **Donovan Hurst**

December 14, 2012

Dedication

This work is dedicated to all of those that came before us and shaped our lives to make us the people that we are today.

Table of Contents

Introduction

This is a compilation of individuals who have the surname of Alexander that lived in the country of Ireland from the 1600s to the 1900s. I have placed each entry into one of four categories: Families, Individual Births/Baptisms, Individual Burials, and Individual Marriages. If a marriage entry primarily concerns an Individual Alexander whom is female, then I have placed that entry under the category of Individual Marriages. If a marriage entry primarily concerns an Individual Alexander whom is male, then I have placed that entry under the category of Families. Images of many of these listings are available at http://churchrecords.irishgenealogy.ie/churchrecords/.

To help guide the reader of this work, the format of this book is as follows:

- Main Family Entry (Husband and Wife) (Father and Mother)

    o Child of Main Family Entry, including Spouse(s) when available

        ▪ Grandchild of Main Family Entry, including Spouse(s) when available

            • Great-Grandchild of Main Family Entry, including Spouse(s) when available

(**Bolded Text**) following any entry includes any additional information such as Residence(s), Occupation(s), Signature(s), etc. when available.

Hurst

Some of the fonts used in this work symbolizes Celtic writing. The traditional letters, numbers, and punctuation marks and their Celtic counterparts are as follows:

Traditional Letters (Uppercase & Lowercase)

A a B b C c D d E f G g H h I i J j K k L l M m N n O o P p Q q R r S s T t U u V v W w X x Y y Z z

Celtic Letters (Uppercase & Lowercase)

A a B b C c D ð E e F f G g H h I í J j K k L l M m

N n O o P p Q q R ʀ S s T t U u V v W w X x Y y Z z

Traditional Numbers

1 2 3 4 5 6 7 8 9 10

Celtic Numbers

1 2 3 4 5 6 7 8 9 10

Traditional Punctuation

. , : ' " & - ( )

Celtic Punctuation

. , : ' " & - ( )

Alexander Surname Ireland: 1600s to 1900s

Parish Churches

Carlow (Church of Ireland)

Carlow Parish, Clonagoose Parish, Clonmelsh Parish, Cloydagh Parish, Dunleckney Parish, Painestown Parish, Painestown - St. Anne Parish, and Wells Parish.

Cork & Ross

(Roman Catholic or RC)

Cork - South Parish and Cork - SS. Peter & Paul Parish.

Dublin (Church of Ireland)

Arbour Hill Barracks Parish, Beggar's Bush Barracks Parish, Clontarf Parish, Harold's Cross Parish, Irishtown Parish, Kilmainham Parish, Milltown Parish, North Strand Parish, Portobello Barracks Parish, Rathmines Parish, Richmond Barracks Parish, Rotunda Chapel Paris, Sandford Parish, South Dublin Union Parish, St. Andrew Parish, St. Anne Parish, St. Audoen Parish, St. Bride Parish, St. Catherine Parish, St. George Parish, St. James Parish, St. John Parish, St. Luke Parish, St. Mark Parish, St. Mary Parish, St. Matthew Parish, St. Mathias Parish, St. Michael Parish, St. Michan Parish, St. Nicholas Within Parish, St. Nicholas Without Parish, St. Patrick Parish, St. Paul Parish, St. Peter Parish, St. Stephen Parish, St. Thomas Parish, St. Werburgh Parish, and Taney Parish.

Dublin (Roman Catholic or RC)

Clondalkin Parish, Harrington Street Parish, Lucan Parish, Rathmines Parish, SS. Michael & John Parish, St. Andrew Parish, St. Audoen Parish, St. Catherine Parish, St. James Parish, St. Mary Parish, St. Mary, Haddington Road Parish, St. Mary, Pro Cathedral Parish, St. Michan Parish, and St. Nicholas Parish.

Kerry (Church of Ireland)

Dingle Parish, Kilcrohane Parish, and Tralee Parish.

Kerry (Roman Catholic or RC)

Tralee Parish.

Families

- Albert Edward Alexander & Elizabeth Alexander

  o Anne Alexander – b. 14 Nov 1886, bapt. 3 Dec 1886 (Baptism, **Richmond Barracks Parish**)

Albert Edward Alexander (father):

Residence - Richmond Barracks - December 3, 1886

Occupation - Lieutenant Corporal 2nd Welsh Regiment - December 3, 1886

- Alexander Alexander & Eleanor Elimore – 18 Oct 1813 (Marriage, **St. James Parish**)

- Alexander Alexander & Ellen Alexander

  o Mary Alexander – bapt. 18 Aug 1819 (Baptism, **St. Mary Parish**)

- Alexander Alexander & Mary Unknown

  o Joseph James Alexander – bapt. Nov 1851 (Baptism, **SS. Michael & John Parish (RC)**)

- Alexander Alexander & Unknown

  o Isabel Alexander – bapt. 4 Aug 1700 (Baptism, **St. Catherine Parish**)

- Alexander Alexander & Unknown

  o James Alexander & Jane White – 5 Apr 1852 (Marriage, **St. Catherine Parish**)

Signatures:

1

Hurst

James Alexander (son):

    Residence - Earl Street - April 5, 1852

    Occupation - Farmer - April 5, 1852

Jane White, daughter of James White (daughter-in-law):

    Residence - Earl Street - April 5, 1852

James White (father):

    Occupation - Farmer

Alexander Alexander (father):

    Occupation - Farmer

Wedding Witnesses:

Thomas White & Jane White

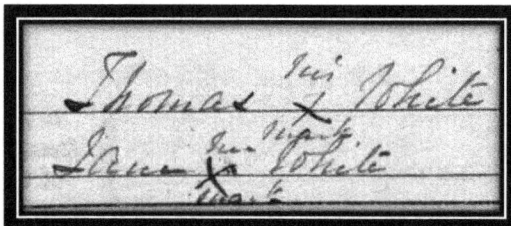

Signatures:

- Alexander Alexander & Winifred Alexander
    - Alexander Alexander – bapt. 18 Sep 1731 (Baptism, St. Catherine Parish)
- Andrew Alexander & Jane McDowell – 24 May 1752 (Marriage, St. Michan Parish)

Alexander Surname Ireland: 1600s to 1900s

- Andrew Alexander & Unknown

  o Andrew Alexander & Jane Purden – 11 Jan 1851 (Marriage, **St. Peter Parish**)

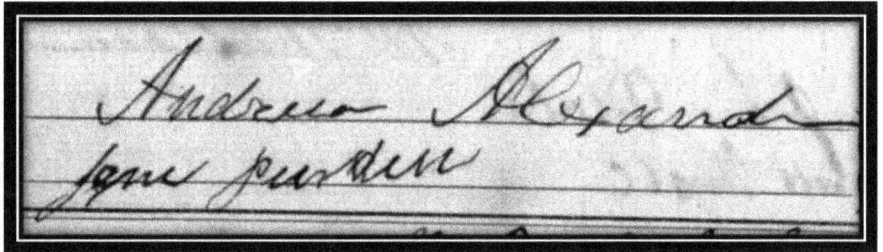

Signatures:

Andrew Alexander (son):

    Residence - 2 Wellington Road - January 11, 1851

    Occupation - Carpenter - January 11, 1851

Jane Purden, daughter of John Purden (daughter-in-law):

    Residence - 2 Wellington Road - January 11, 1851

John Purden (father):

    Occupation - Laborer

Andrew Alexander (father):

    Occupation - Stone Mason

Hurst

Wedding Witnesses:

Bernard O'Brien & Margaret Jane Booth

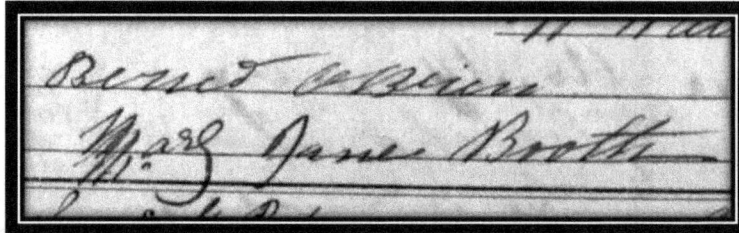

Signatures:

- Anthony Alexander, bur. 25 Aug 1789 (Burial, **St. John Parish**) & Mary Unknown

  - Sarah Alexander – bapt. 23 Oct 1768 (Baptism, **St. John Parish**)

  - Margaret Alexander – bapt. 1 Apr 1770 (Baptism, **St. John Parish**)

  - Thomas Alexander – bapt. 1 May 1775 (Baptism, **St. John Parish**)

- Cannell Alexander & Rose Alexander

  - Caroline Alexander – bapt. 15 Jan 1836 (Baptism, **St. Mary, Pro Cathedral Parish (RC)**)

- Charles Alexander & Catherine Blanchfield

  - Elizabeth Alexander – b. 15 Mar 1873, bapt. 16 Apr 1873 (Baptism, **St. Mary, Pro Cathedral Parish (RC)**)

Charles Alexander (father):

Residence - 15 Talbot Street - April 16, 1873

- Charles Alexander & Catherine Unknown

  - Charles Alexander – bapt. 8 Jun 1757 (Baptism, **St. Michan Parish (RC)**)

Alexander Surname Ireland: 1600s to 1900s

- Charles Alexander & Lucy Alexander

  o Kathleen Mary Alexander – b. 5 Sep 1894, bapt. 28 Sep 1894 (Baptism, **Beggar's Bush Barracks Parish**)

Charles Alexander (father):

  Residence - Beggar's Bush Barracks - September 28, 1894

  Occupation - Bandsman 2nd D C LT - September 28, 1894

- Charles Alexander & Unknown

Signature:

  o Godfrey E. Alexander & Harriet Alexander Shaw – 10 Oct 1850 (Marriage, **St. George Parish**)

Signatures:

Godfrey E. Alexander (son):

  Residence - Calidor, Co. Tyrone - October 10, 1850

  Occupation - Clerk - October 10, 1850

Harriet Alexander Shaw, daughter of William John Alexander Shaw (daughter-in-law):

Hurst

Residence - Belvidere Place - October 10, 1850

William John Alexander Shaw (father):

Signature:

Occupation - Gentleman

Charles Alexander (father):

Occupation - Clerk

Wedding Witnesses:

William John Alexander Shaw & Robert Quinn Alexander

Signatures:

- Charles Alexander & Unknown
  - Jessie Alexander & William Jones – 15 Feb 1851 (Marriage, George Parish)

Signatures:

Jessie Alexander (daughter):

Residence - 8 Summerhill Parade - February 15, 1851

Alexander Surname Ireland: 1600s to 1900s

William Jones, son of John Jones (son-in-law):

Residence - 36 Summer Street North - February 15, 1851

Occupation - Tradesman - February 15, 1851

Relationship Status at Marriage - widow

John Jones (father):

Occupation - Builder

Charles Alexander (father):

Occupation - Farmer

Wedding Witnesses:

David Alexander & Margaret Goyder

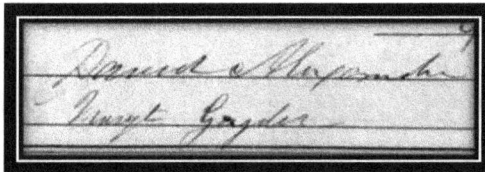

Signatures:

- Christopher Alexander & Elizabeth Unknown

  o Jane Alexander – bapt. 18 Aug 1738 (Baptism, **St. Peter Parish**)

- David Alexander & Anne Powell – 5 Sep 1839 (Marriage, **St. Peter Parish**)

David Alexander (husband):

Residence - Lower Abbey Street, St. Thomas Parish - September 5, 1839

Anne Powell (wife):

Residence - Ranelagh - September 5, 1839

Hurst

- David Alexander & Hold Hugu – 6 May 1719 (Marriage, **St. Michael Parish**)

- David Alexander & Unknown

  o James Hutchinson Alexander & Agnes Willey – 27 May 1896 (Marriage, **St. Werburgh Parish**)

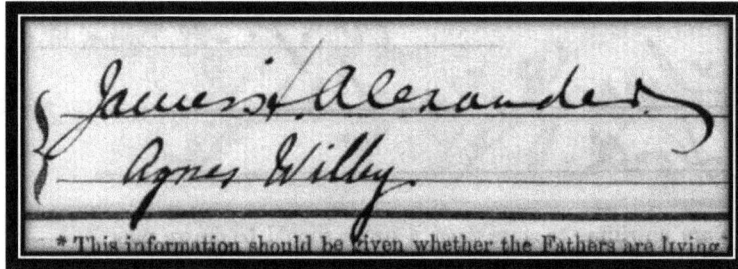

Signatures:

- Alfred James Alexander – b. 27 Feb 1897, bapt. 28 Mar 1897 (Baptism, **St. Werburgh Parish**)

James Hutchinson Alexander (son):

Residence - 14 Grafton Street - May 27, 1896

3 Leeson Park Avenue - March 28, 1897

Occupation - Book Keeper - May 27, 1896

March 28, 1897

Agnes Willey, daughter of Thomas James Willey (daughter-in-law):

Residence - 24 South Great George Street - May 27, 1896

Thomas James Willey (father):

Occupation - Printer

Alexander Surname Ireland: 1600s to 1900s

David Alexander (father):

    Occupation - Military Officer

Wedding Witnesses:

Charles Hinds & Elizabeth Willey

Signatures:

- David A. Alexander & Unknown
    - David McGowan Alexander & Emily Frances Gahagan – 17 Sep 1873 (Marriage, **St. Thomas Parish**)

Signature:

Signatures (Marriage):

Hurst

- Olive Lissette Alexander – b. 18 Jul 1882, bapt. 10 Aug 1882 (Baptism, **St. Peter Parish**)

- Charles Henry Alexander – b. 29 Dec 1883, bapt. 7 Feb 1884 (Baptism, **St. Peter Parish**)

- Eileen Grace Alexander – b. 25 Oct 1885, bapt. 15 Dec 1885 (Baptism, **St. Peter Parish**)

- Winifred Alexander – b. 8 Dec 1886, bapt. 25 Jan 1887 (Baptism, **St. Peter Parish**)

- Harold Gilbert Alexander – b. 4 Jan 1889, bapt. 21 Mar 1889 (Baptism, **St. Peter Parish**)

- Grace Howard Alexander – b. 17 Jun 1891, bapt. 16 Jul 1891 (Baptism, **St. Peter Parish**)

David McGowan Alexander (son):

Residence - 109 Seville Place - September 17, 1873

86 Rathmines Road - August 10, 1882

February 7, 1884

December 15, 1885

January 25, 1887

71 Frankfort Avenue - March 21, 1889

July 16, 1891

Occupation - Lithographer - September 17, 1873

August 10, 1882

February 7, 1884

December 15, 1885

January 25, 1887

March 21, 1889

July 16, 1891

Emily Frances Gahagan, daughter of Francis P. Gahagan (daughter-in-law):

Residence - 2 Beresford Place - September 17, 1873

Francis P. Gahagan (father):

Occupation - Hotel Keeper

David A. Alexander (father):

Occupation - Royal Artillery

Wedding Witnesses:

John Richard Gahagan & Charles Alexander

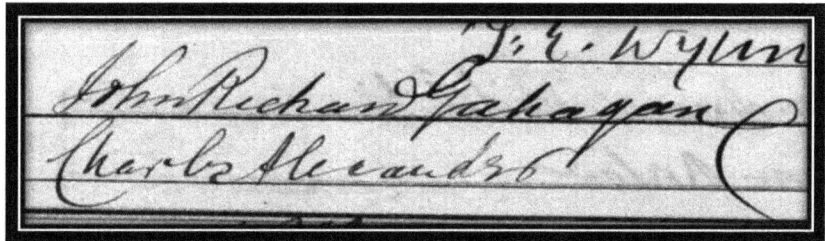

Signatures:

- Edmund Alexander & Linnet Catherine Unknown

  - Robert Alexander – bapt. 2 Feb 1796 (Baptism, SS. Michael & John Parish (RC))

Edmund Alexander (father):

Residence - Old Custom House - February 2, 1796

- Francis Alexander & Mary Donovan

  - George Alexander – bapt. 17 Feb 1797 (Baptism, Cork - SS. Peter & Paul Parish (RC))

Francis Alexander (father):

Residence - Back Shambles - February 17, 1797

- Frederick William Nassau Alexander, b. 1777, bur. 29 May 1852 (Burial, **St. Werburgh Parish**) (1st Marriage) & Rebecca Unknown, bur. 9 Mar 1829 (Burial, **St. Werburgh Parish**)

  o Margaret Jane Alexander – bapt. 3 Dec 1815 (Baptism, **St. Werburgh Parish**), bur. 1 Nov 1822 (Burial, **St. Werburgh Parish**)

Margaret Jane Alexander (daughter):

Residence - 12 Castle Street - before November 1, 1822

Age at Death - 8 years

  o Eleanor Sarah Alexander – b. 28 Sep 1817, bapt. 5 Oct 1817 (Baptism, **St. Werburgh Parish**)

  o Rebecca Alexander, b. 28 Sep 1817, bapt. 5 Oct 1817 (Baptism, **St. Werburgh Parish**) & Thomas Grantham Atkinson – 1 Oct 1847 (Marriage, **George Parish**)

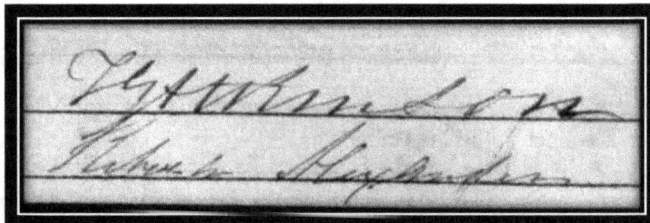

Signatures:

Rebecca Alexander (daughter):

Residence - 36 Nelson Street - October 1, 1847

Thomas Grantham Atkinson, son of William Atkinson (son-in-law):

Residence - Naas, Co. Kildare - October 1, 1847

Occupation - Gentleman - October 1, 1847

Relationship Status at Marriage - widow

Alexander Surname Ireland: 1600s to 1900s

William Atkinson (father):

    Occupation - Gentleman

Frederick William Nassau Alexander (father):

    Occupation - Gentleman

Wedding Witnesses:

Frederick Alexander & Thomas Ferrall

Signatures:

- Eleanor Alexander – b. 28 Feb 1819, bapt. 7 Mar 1819 (Baptism, **St. Werburgh Parish**)

- Sarah Alexander – b. 21 May 1820, bapt. 28 May 1820 (Baptism, **St. Werburgh Parish**)

- Robert Banks Alexander – b. 30 Sep 1821, bapt. 14 Oct 1821 (Baptism, **St. Werburgh Parish**)

- Frederick William Nassau Alexander – b. 14 Feb 1823, bapt. 23 Feb 1823 (Baptism, **St. Werburgh Parish**), bur. 2 Jul 1823 (Burial, **St. Werburgh Parish**)

Frederick William Nassau Alexander (son):

Residence - 12 Castle Street - before July 2, 1823

Age at Death - 4 ½ months

Hurst

- ○ John Cassin Alexander – b. 23 May 1824, bapt. 1 Jun 1824 (Baptism, **St. Werburgh Parish**)

- ○ Mary Anne Alexander, b. 28 Sep 1825, bapt. 20 Oct 1825 (Baptism, **St. Werburgh Parish**) & Matthew Jackson – 24 Feb 1849 (Marriage, **St. Andrew Parish**)

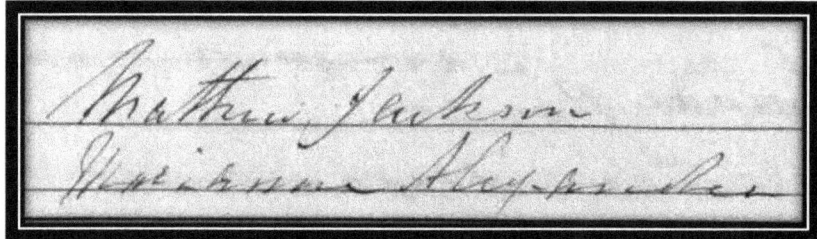

Signatures:

Mary Anne Alexander (daughter):

  Residence - 88 South Great George's Street - February 24, 1849

Matthew Jackson, son of William Jackson (son-in-law):

  Residence - Wenderry - February 24, 1849

  Occupation - Gentleman - February 24, 1849

  Relationship Status at Marriage - widow

William Jackson (father):

  Occupation - Gentleman

Frederick William Nassau Alexander (father):

  Occupation - Gentleman

Alexander Surname Ireland: 1600s to 1900s

Wedding Witnesses:

Frederick Alexander & Thomas Ferrall

Signatures:

- Martha Elizabeth Alexander – b. 5 Oct 1827, bapt. 14 Oct 1827 (Baptism, **St. Werburgh Parish**)

Frederick William Nassau Alexander (father) (1st Marriage):

Residence - 12 Castle Street - December 3, 1815

October 5, 1817

March 7, 1819

May 28, 1820

October 14, 1821

February 23, 1823

October 14, 1827

No. 36 Nelson Street - before May 29, 1852

Age at Death - 75 years

Rebecca Unknown (mother):

Age at Death - 42 years

Hurst

- Frederick William Nassau Alexander, b. 1777, bur. 29 May 1852 (Burial, **St. Werburgh Parish**) (2nd Marriage) & Harriet Trousdell – 27 Aug 1831 (Marriage, **St. Werburgh Parish**)

Signatures:

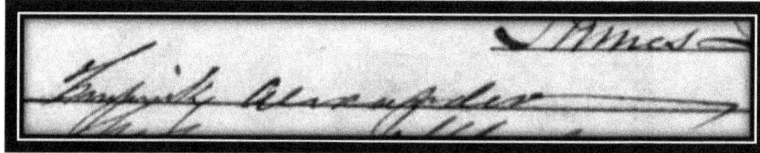

Signatures (Marriage):

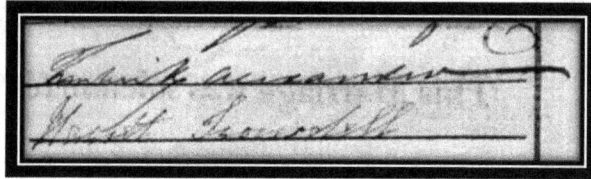

- Harriet Alexander – bur. 1832 (Burial, **St. Werburgh Parish**)

Harriet Alexander (daughter):

Residence - Castle Street - before 1832

- Frederick William Nassau Alexander – b. 20 Aug 1832, bapt. 9 Sep 1832 (Baptism, **St. Werburgh Parish**)
- Sarah Louisa Alexander – b. 5 Sep 1833, bapt. 29 Sep 1833 (Baptism, **St. Werburgh Parish**)
- William Brown Alexander – b. 15 Oct 1835, bapt. 1 Nov 1835 (Baptism, **St. Werburgh Parish**)
- Anne Fawcett Alexander – b. 5 May 1837, bapt. 21 May 1837 (Baptism, **St. Werburgh Parish**), bur. 28 Nov 1844 (Burial, **St. Werburgh Parish**)

Alexander Surname Ireland: 1600s to 1900s

Anne Fawcett Alexander (daughter):

Residence - Queen's Street - before November 28, 1844

Age at Death - 8 years

- Frances Brown Alexander – b. 16 Mar 1839, bapt. 26 Apr 1839 (Baptism, **St. Werburgh Parish**), bur. 26 Nov 1844 (Burial, **St. Werburgh Parish**)

Frances Brown Alexander (daughter):

Residence - Queen's Street - before November 26, 1844

Age at Death - 6 years

- Mary Margaret Trousdell Alexander – b. 22 Oct 1840, bapt. 3 Nov 1840 (Baptism, **St. Werburgh Parish**)
- Elizabeth Catherine Fannin Alexander – b. 21 Oct 1841, bapt. 31 Dec 1841 (Baptism, **St. Werburgh Parish**), bur. 20 Nov 1844 (Burial, **St. Werburgh Parish**)

Elizabeth Catherine Fannin Alexander (daughter):

Residence - Queen's Street - before November 20, 1844

Age at Death - 3 years

- Thomas Ferrall Alexander – b. 2 Jan 1849, bapt. 26 Jan 1849 (Baptism, **St. George Parish**)
- Harriet Alexander – b. 2 Mar 1850, bapt. 24 Mar 1850 (Baptism, **St. George Parish**)

Frederick William Nassau Alexander (father) (2nd Marriage):

Residence - St. Werburgh Parish - August 27, 1831

No. 36 Nelson Street - January 26, 1849

Hurst

March 24, 1850

before May 29, 1852

Occupation - Gentleman - January 26, 1849

March 24, 1850

Age at Death - 75 years

Harriet Trousdell (mother):

Residence - St. Werburgh Parish - August 27, 1831

Wedding Witnesses:

William Trousdell & William Smith

Signatures:

- Frederick Alexander & Unknown
  - Catherine Elizabeth Alexander & William Rock – 22 Jan 1871 (Marriage, St. Audoen Parish)

Signatures:

Alexander Surname Ireland: 1600s to 1900s

Catherine Elizabeth Alexander (daughter):

   Residence - Armagh - January 22, 1871

William Rock, son of Richard Rock (son-in-law):

   Residence - 41 Nicholas Street - January 22, 1871

   Occupation - Mercantile Clerk - January 22, 1871

Richard Rock (father):

Signature:

   Occupation - Watch & Clock Maker

Frederick Alexander (father):

   Occupation - Merchant

Wedding Witnesses:

Richard Rock & Elizabeth Jane Rock

Signatures:

- George Alexander & Alberta Hughes

  o Eva Emily Alexander – b. 1877, bapt. 1898 (Baptism, **St. Andrew Parish (RC)**)

  o John Alexander – b. 6 Nov 1888, bapt. 16 Jan 1889 (Baptism, **St. George Parish**)

Hurst

George Alexander (father):

Residence - 4 Richmond Terrace - January 16, 1889

10 Nassau Place - 1898

Occupation - Police Pensioner - January 16, 1889

- George Alexander & Honor Fagan

  o Michael Alexander – bapt. 9 Nov 1803 (Baptism, **St. Michan Parish** (RC))

- George Alexander & Jane Alexander

  o John Alexander – bapt. 24 Apr 1734 (Baptism, **St. Mark Parish**)

  o Elizabeth Alexander – bapt. 11 Nov 1736 (Baptism, **St. Mark Parish**)

- George Alexander & Jane Byrne (B y r n e)

  o Georgina Mary Alexander – b. 13 May 1892, bapt. 6 Jun 1892 (Baptism, **St. Mary, Haddington Road Parish** (RC))

George Alexander (father):

Residence - 45 Shelbourne Road - June 6, 1892

- George Alexander & Mary Hughes

  o Eva Emma Alexander – b. 4 Apr 1875, bapt. 30 Apr 1875 (Baptism, **St. Mary, Pro Cathedral Parish** (RC))

George Alexander (father):

Residence - Ennis - April 30, 1875

Alexander Surname Ireland: 1600s to 1900s

- George Alexander & Mary Nolan – 15 Jun 1841 (Marriage, **St. Michan Parish (RC)**)

    o Anne Alexander – bapt. 1 Apr 1842 (Baptism, **St. Nicholas Parish (RC)**)

    o Jane Alexander – bapt. 14 Dec 1846 (Baptism, **St. Nicholas Parish (RC)**)

    o George Alexander – bapt. 14 Nov 1848 (Baptism, **St. Nicholas Parish (RC)**)

    o Mary Alexander, bapt. 22 Jun 1853 (Baptism, **St. Nicholas Parish (RC)**) & Maurice Malone – 2 Jul 1871 (Marriage, **St. Nicholas Parish (RC)**)

Mary Alexander (daughter):

Residence - 34 Golden Lane - July 2, 1871

Maurice Malone, son of George Malone & Anne Unknown (son-in-law):

Residence - 20 Whitefriar Street - July 2, 1871

Wedding Witnesses:

Thomas Tilson & Catherine Malone

    o Catherine Alexander – b. 9 Jul 1857, bapt. 13 Jul 1857 (Baptism, **St. Nicholas Parish (RC)**)

George Alexander (father):

Residence - 15 Golden Lane - July 13, 1857

- George Alexander & Unknown

    o Joseph Alexander & Mary Ashe – 25 Oct 1850 (Marriage, **St. Paul Parish**)

Signatures:

Hurst

Joseph Alexander (son):

    Residence - Mount Pelier Hill - October 25, 1850

    Occupation - Gentleman - October 25, 1850

Mary Ashe, daughter of William Sands Ashe (daughter-in-law):

    Residence - Mount Pelier Hill - October 25, 1850

William Sands Ashe (father):

    Occupation - Clergyman

George Alexander (father);

    Occupation - Gentleman

Wedding Witnesses:

William Thomas Ashe & Anne Lowen

Signatures:

Alexander Surname Ireland: 1600s to 1900s

- George Alexander & Unknown

  o George Alexander & Emily Louisa Brooks – 9 Jan 1884 (Marriage, **Milltown Parish**)

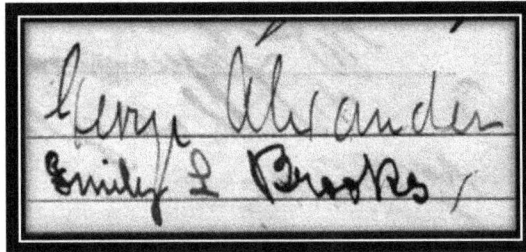

Signatures:

George Alexander (son):

    Residence - Weston Park, Leixlip - January 9, 1884

    Occupation - Farmer - January 9, 1884

Emily Louisa Brooks, daughter of John Brooks (daughter-in-law):

    Residence - Alston Temple Road Rathmines - January 9, 1884

John Brooks (father):

    Occupation - Merchant

George Alexander (father):

    Occupation - Farmer

Wedding Witnesses:

Maurice Brooks & William A. Walk

Signatures:

- George Washington Alexander & Hannah Unknown

  o George Muirhead Alexander – b. 16 Sep 1896, bapt. 18 Oct 1896 (Baptism, **St. James Parish**)

George Washington Alexander (father):

Residence - Rutland Villa, Dolphin's Barn - October 18, 1896

Occupation - Confectioner - October 18, 1896

- Gulielmo Alexander & Mary Byrne (B y r n e)

  o Gulielmo Joseph Alexander – b. 26 Apr 1880, bapt. 3 May 1880 (Baptism, **St. Mary, Haddington Road Parish (RC)**)

  o Mary Josephine Alexander – b. 2 Jun 1882, bapt. 12 Jun 1882 (Baptism, **St. Mary, Haddington Road Parish (RC)**)

  o Elizabeth Josephine Alexander – b. 9 Apr 1885, bapt. 13 Apr 1885 (Baptism, **St. Mary, Haddington Road Parish (RC)**)

Alexander Surname Ireland: 1600s to 1900s

Gulielmo Alexander (father):

    Residence - 6 Eastmoreland Lane - May 3, 1880

        13 Haddington Road - June 12, 1882

        10 Haddington Road - April 13, 1885

- Henry Alexander & Unknown
  - Margaret Alexander & Samuel Gibney – 17 Apr 1876 (Marriage, **St. Mark Parish**)

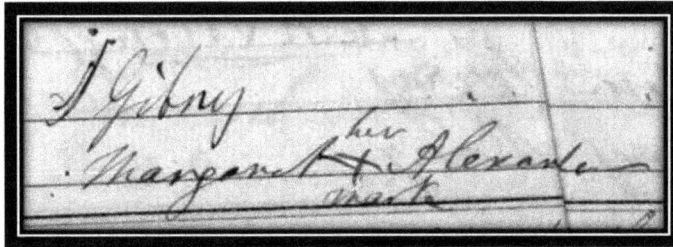

Signatures:

Margaret Alexander (daughter):

    Residence - 27 Great Clarence Street - April 17, 1876

Samuel Gibney, son of Michael Gibney (son-in-law):

    Residence - 27 Great Clarence Street - April 17, 1876

    Occupation - Bricklayer - April 17, 1876

Michael Gibney (father):

    Occupation - Bricklayer

Henry Alexander (father):

    Occupation - Farmer

Hurst

Wedding Witnesses:

Thomas William Higgins & George Bradford

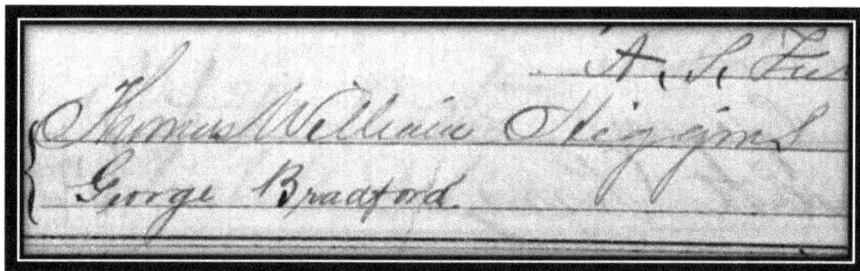

Signatures:

- Henry Clement Alexander & Kathleen O'Brien

  ○ Edward James Alexander – b. 23 Apr 1887, bapt. 4 May 1887 (Baptism, **St. Michan Parish (RC)**)

Henry Clement Alexander (father):

Residence - 8 Dargle Road, Drumcondra - May 4, 1887

- Hugh Alexander & Alice Kelley – 1 Jun 1794 (Marriage, **St. Bride Parish**)

Hugh Alexander (husband):

Occupation - Gentleman - June 1, 1794

- Hugh Alexander & Ellen Egan

  ○ David Alexander – b. 27 Mar 1871, bapt. 2 Apr 1871 (Baptism, **Cork - SS. Peter & Paul Parish (RC)**)

Alexander Surname Ireland: 1600s to 1900s

- Hugh Alexander & Ellen Nagle

  o Mary Ellen Alexander – b. 10 May 1873, bapt. 18 May 1873 (Baptism, **Cork - SS. Peter & Paul Parish (RC)**)

  o Christopher Alexander Alexander – b. 25 Dec 1876, bapt. 25 Dec 1876 (Baptism, **Cork - SS. Peter & Paul Parish (RC)**)

  o Isabel Alexander – b. 7 Dec 1879, bapt. 14 Dec 1879 (Baptism, **Cork - SS. Peter & Paul Parish (RC)**)

- James Alexander & Agnes Alexander

  o Violet Agnes Alexander – b. 1898, bapt. 1898 (Baptism, **Sandford Parish**)

James Alexander (father):

Residence - 8 Lower Beechwood Avenue - 1898

Occupation - Bookkeeper - 1898

- James Alexander & Anne Alexander

  o Elizabeth Alexander – bapt. 27 Apr 1794 (Baptism, **St. Mary Parish**)

James Alexander (father):

Residence - Abbey Street - April 27, 1794

- James Alexander & Anne Alexander

  o Catherine Alexander – bapt. 1 Dec 1805 (Baptism, **St. Mark Parish**)

James Alexander (father):

Residence - 40 Fleet Street - December 1, 1805

Hurst

- James Alexander & Anne Unknown

  - Elizabeth Alexander – bapt. 29 Jul 1776 (Baptism, **St. Peter Parish**)

- James Alexander & Barbara Alexander

  - Anne Alexander – bapt. 5 Jan 1734 (Baptism, **St. Mary Parish**)

  - Mary Alexander – bapt. 1 Jan 1737 (Baptism, **St. Mary Parish**)

  - Barbara Alexander – b. 24 Mar 1745, bapt. 12 Apr 1746 (Baptism, **St. Mary Parish**)

- James Alexander & Catherine Reynolds – 21 Feb 1811 (Marriage, **St. Peter Parish**)

- James Alexander & Ellen McCarthy – 7 Nov 1850 (Marriage, **Cork - South Parish** (RC))

Wedding Witnesses:

Susan Alexander & Mary Barrett

- James Alexander & Hannah Alexander

  - Elizabeth Alexander – bapt. 28 Nov 1776 (Baptism, **St. Mary Parish**)

- James Alexander & Jane Alexander

  - James Alexander – b. 1808, bapt. 10 Jan 1808 (Baptism, **Carlow Parish**)

- James Alexander & Mary Byrne (B y r n e)

  - Nicholas Alexander – bapt. 28 May 1822 (Baptism, **St. Catherine Parish** (RC))

- James Alexander & Sarah Daugherty – 20 Nov 1763 (Marriage, **St. Michan Parish** (RC))

- James Alexander & Toaima [Hard to Read] Unknown

  - Jane Alexander – bapt. 26 Mar 1725 (Baptism, **St. Paul Parish**)

- James Alexander & Unknown

  - Mary Alexander – bur. 27 Sep 1704 (Baptism, **St. John Parish**)

Alexander Surname Ireland: 1600s to 1900s

- James Alexander & Unknown

  o Martha Alexander & Henry Smith – 16 Jul 1860 (Marriage, **St. Thomas Parish**)

Signatures:

Martha Alexander (daughter):

  Residence - 11 Amiens Street - July 16, 1860

Henry Smith, son of James Smith (son-in-law):

  Residence - 11 Amiens Street - July 16, 1860

  Occupation - Merchant - July 16, 1860

James Smith (father):

  Occupation - Merchant

James Alexander (father):

  Occupation - Merchant

Wedding Witnesses:

Sarah Robinson & Thomas Jones

Signatures:

- James Alexander & Unknown

  o Mary Susan Caroline Alexander & James Frederick Mahon – 5 Dec 1872 (Marriage, **George Parish**)

Signatures:

Mary Susan Caroline Alexander (daughter):

Residence - 3 North Richmond Street - December 5, 1872

James Frederick Mahon, son of George Mahon (son-in-law):

Residence - Palmerston Place, St. Mary Parish - December 5, 1872

Occupation - Gentleman - December 5, 1872

Alexander Surname Ireland: 1600s to 1900s

George Mahon (father):

    Occupation - Medical Doctor

James Alexander (father):

    Occupation - Esquire

Wedding Signatures:

David Laynmor & Henry Mahon

Signatures:

- James Alexander & Unknown
  - Joseph Alexander & Ellen McDonald Kelly – 11 Feb 1873 (Marriage, **St. Paul Parish**)

Signatures:

Joseph Alexander (son):

    Residence - Royal Barracks - February 11, 1873

    Occupation - Private in PT Royal Dragoons - February 11, 1873

Hurst

Ellen MacDonald Kelly, daughter of Alexander McDonald (daughter-in-law):

    Residence - 20 Barrack Street - February 11, 1873

    Relationship Status at Marriage - widow

Alexander McDonald (father):

    Occupation - Smith

James Alexander (father):

    Occupation - Bootmaker

Wedding Witnesses:

James Hayes & Mary Durham

Signatures:

- James Edward Alexander & Evelyn Mary Alexander
  - Gerald D'Arragon Alexander – bapt. 20 Apr 1859 (Baptism, **Arbour Hill Barracks Parish**)

James Edward Alexander (father):

    Residence - 17 Mount Pelier Hill - April 20, 1859

    Occupation - Colonel 2 Battalion, 14th Regiment - April 20, 1859

Alexander Surname Ireland: 1600s to 1900s

- Jeremiah Alexander & Unknown

  - Jeremiah Alexander – bapt. 13 Jun 1630 (Baptism, **St. John Parish**)

  - William Alexander – bapt. 10 Jan 1632 (Baptism, **St. John Parish**)

  - John Alexander – bapt. 11 Mar 1633 (Baptism, **St. John Parish**)

- John Alexander & Anne Alexander

  - Anne Alexander – bapt. 5 Feb 1792 (Baptism, **St. Mary Parish**)

John Alexander (father):

Residence - Swift's Row - February 5, 1792

- John Alexander & Anne Dowling

  - Richard Alexander – bapt. 1820 (Baptism, **St. Mary Parish (RC)**)

- John Alexander & Anne O'Neill – 8 Apr 1839 (Marriage, **St. Nicholas Within Parish**) (Marriage, **St. Nicholas Parish (RC)**)

  - Edward John Alexander – bapt. 15 Mar 1841 (Baptism, **St. Nicholas Parish (RC)**)

John Alexander (husband):

Occupation - Police Force - April 8, 1839

- John Alexander & Bridget Jugdunce – 25 May 1835 (Marriage, **St. Andrew Parish (RC)**)

- John Alexander & Catherine Clifford – 19 Dec 1727 (Marriage, **St. Werburgh Parish**)

- John Alexander & Catherine Egan – 15 Apr 1699 (Marriage, **St. Peter Parish**)

- John Alexander & Catherine Kerr

  - Mary Alexander – bapt. 1842 (Baptism, **St. Mary Parish (RC)**)

Hurst

- John Alexander & Catherine Killeen

  - Gulielmo Alexander & Mary Byrne (B y r n e) – 27 Nov 1869 (Marriage, **Rathmines Parish (RC)**)

Gulielmo Alexander (son):

Residence - Haddington Road - November 27, 1869

Mary Byrne, daughter of John Byrne & Anne Madden (daughter-in-law):

Residence -Mount Pleasant - November 27, 1869

- John Alexander & Elizabeth Alexander

  - Thomas Alexander – bapt. 4 Apr 1757 (Baptism, **St. Mark Parish**)

John Alexander (father):

Residence - Hawkin's Quay - April 4, 1757

- John Alexander & Elizabeth Alexander

  - William Alexander – bapt. 14 Nov 1829 (Baptism, **St. Mary, Pro Cathedral Parish (RC)**)

John Alexander (father):

Residence - Townsend Street - November 14, 1829

- John Alexander & Elizabeth Mason – 6 Jan 1791 (Marriage, **St. Peter Parish**)
- John Alexander & Elizabeth Unknown

  - Anne Alexander – bapt. 8 Jul 1733 (Baptism, **St. Audoen Parish**)

  - Jane Alexander – bapt. 17 Sep 1734 (Baptism, **St. Audoen Parish**)

  - Anne Alexander – bapt. 21 Jun 1736 (Baptism, **St. Audoen Parish**)

Alexander Surname Ireland: 1600s to 1900s

- ○ Fargis Alexander – bapt. 31 Jul 1738 (Baptism, **St. Audoen Parish**)

- ○ Unknown Alexander – bapt. 6 Jan 1739 (Baptism, **St. Audoen Parish**)

- • John Alexander & Elizabeth Jane Alexander

- ○ Eugenie Maude Josephine Alexander – b. 17 Oct 1859, bapt. 2 Nov 1859 (Baptism, **St. Peter Parish**)

John Alexander (father):

Residence - 6 Wentworth Terrace - November 2, 1859

Occupation - Commercial Traveller - November 2, 1859

- • John Alexander, b. 1801, bur. 14 Oct 1885 (Burial, **Cloydagh Parish**) & Esther Alexander

Signatures:

- ○ Harriet Lucy Alexander & Edward George Moore Donnithorne (D o n n i t h o r n e) – 8 Jul 1875 (Marriage, **Cloydagh Parish**)

Signatures:

Harriet Lucy Alexander (daughter):

    Residence - Milford - July 8, 1875

Edward George Moore Donnithorne, son of Edward Harris Donnithorne

(son-in-law):

    Residence - Cluc Lodge, Twickenham - July 8, 1875

    Occupation - Captain Scots Greys - July 8, 1875

Edward Harris Donnithorne (father):

    Occupation - Gentleman

John Alexander (father):

    Occupation - Gentleman

Wedding Witnesses:

John Alexander, Edith Longfield, John Alexander Jr. & Esther Alexander

Signatures:

- ○ William Cranston Alexander & Edith Caroline Longfield – 6 Feb 1879 (Marriage, **St. Stephen Parish**)

Signature:

Signatures (Marriage):

William Cranston Alexander (son):

Residence - 4 Victoria Terrace, Upper Leeson Street - February 6, 1879

Occupation - Esquire - February 6, 1879

Edith Caroline Longfield, daughter of William Longfield (daughter-in-law):

Residence - 34 Elgin Road - February 6, 1879

William Longfield (father):

Occupation - Esquire

John Alexander (father):

Occupation - Esquire

Hurst

Wedding Witnesses:

Philip H, Ba -- & George Alexander

Signatures:

- ○ George Alexander & Louisa Bayley – 2 Feb 1891 (Marriage, **Kilmainham Parish**)

Signatures:

- ▪ Albertha Eleanor Alexander – b. 19 Nov 1891, bapt. Feb 1892 (Baptism, **Cloydagh Parish**)

George Alexander (son):

Residence - Sevensaks Inchicore - February 2, 1891

Milford - February 1892

Occupation - Barrister at Law - February 2, 1891

February 1892

Louisa Bayley, daughter of Kenneth Bayley (daughter-in-law):

Residence - Sevensaks Inchicore - February 2, 1891

Kenneth Bayley (father):

Signature:

    Occupation - Chief Engineer G S J W Railway

John Alexander (father):

    Occupation - Gentleman

Wedding Witnesses:

Kenneth Bayley & John Alexander

Signatures:

Hurst

o   John Alexander & Ethel Bayley – 22 Apr 1896 (Marriage, **Kilmainham Parish**)

Signature:

Signatures (Marriage):

- ▪ Jane Alexander – b. 7 Mar 1897, bapt. 4 Apr 1897 (Baptism, **Cloydagh Parish**)

- ▪ John Alexander – b. 9 Jul 1898, bapt. 31 Jul 1898 (Baptism, **Cloydagh Parish**)

- ▪ Kenneth Alexander – b. 23 Mar 1900, bapt. 27 May 1900 (Baptism, **Cloydagh Parish**)

John Alexander (son):

Residence - Milford House, Carlow - April 22, 1896

April 4, 1897

July 31, 1898

May 27, 1900

Occupation - Gentleman - April 22, 1896

Gentleman, Ex Major 11ᵗʰ Hussars - April 4, 1897

July 31, 1898

May 27, 1900

Ethel Bayley, daughter of Kenneth Bayley (daughter-in-law):

Residence - Sevensakes Inchicore - April 22, 1896

Kenneth Bayley (father):

Signature:

Occupation - Chief Engineer G S J W Railway

John Alexander (father):

Occupation - Gentleman

Wedding Witnesses:

Kenneth Bayley & William Alexander

Signatures:

John Alexander (father):

Residence - Milford - before October 14, 1885

Age at Death - 84 Years

Hurst

- John Alexander & Jane Byrne (B y r n e) – 20 Oct 1861 (Marriage, **St. Mary Parish** (RC))

  - Catherine Alexander – bapt. 1862 (Baptism, **St. Mary Parish** (RC))

  - Anne Alexander – bapt. 1865 (Baptism, **St. Mary Parish** (RC))

Wedding Witnesses:

Michael Whelan & Anne Byrne

- John Alexander & Jane Murphy

  - Frances Alexander – b. 1 Nov 1853, bapt. 16 Nov 1853 (Baptism, **St. Mary, Pro Cathedral Parish** (RC))

John Alexander (father):

Residence - 23 Britain Street - November 16, 1853

- John Alexander & Jane Reynolds – 7 Oct 1823 (Marriage, **St. Mary Parish**)

Signatures:

John Alexander (husband):

Residence - Kellenvoy, Co. Roscommon - October 7, 1823

Jane Reynolds (wife):

Residence - St. Mary Parish, Co. Dublin - October 7, 1823

Alexander Surname Ireland: 1600s to 1900s

Wedding Witnesses:

Michael Reynolds & Richard Reynolds

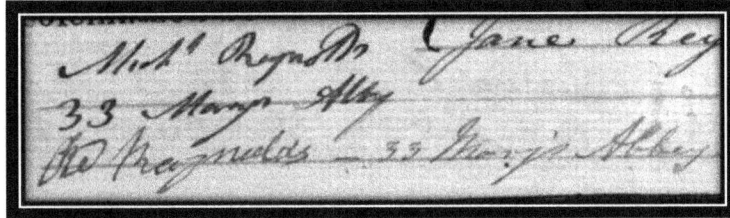

Signatures:

- John Alexander & Josephine Dunbar – 23 Jul 1851 (Marriage, **St. Mary Parish** (RC))

- John Alexander & Judith Larkin – 24 Oct 1760 (Marriage, **St. Paul Parish**)

- John Alexander & Margaret Kenny

  o Charles Alexander – bapt. 31 Oct 1813 (Baptism, **SS. Michael & John Parish** (RC))

- John Alexander & Margaret Unknown

  o George Alexander – bapt. 30 Apr 1764 (Baptism, **St. Audoen Parish**)

- John Alexander & Margaret Unknown

  o Josh Alexander – bapt. 11 Oct 1817 (Baptism, **St. Mary, Pro Cathedral Parish** (RC))

  o Michael Alexander – bapt. 3 Oct 1820 (Baptism, **St. Mary, Pro Cathedral Parish** (RC))

John Alexander (father):

Residence - Coombe - October 11, 1817

October 3, 1820

- John Alexander & Martha Bell – 3 Sep 1776 (Marriage, **St. Mark Parish**)

- John Alexander & Mary Alexander

  o Jane Alexander – b. 4 Jan 1824, bapt. 18 Jan 1824 (Baptism, **St. Werburgh Parish**)

Hurst

- John Alexander & Mary Alexander

  o Edward Alexander – b. 3 Mar 1838, bapt. 10 Jun 1838 (Baptism, **St. Luke Parish**)

John Alexander (father):

Residence - 113 Coombe - June 10, 1838

Occupation - Police Man - June 10, 1838

- John Alexander & Mary Brannon

  o John Alexander – bapt. 29 Jan 1833 (Baptism, **St. Catherine Parish (RC)**)

- John Alexander & Mary Donohoe

  o William Alexander – b. 1811, bapt. 1811 (Baptism, **St. Mary Parish (RC)**)

- John Alexander & Mary Donohoe – 24 Aug 1846 (Marriage, **St. Mary Parish (RC)**)

  o John Alexander & Catherine Henderson – 16 Jan 1893 (Marriage, **St. Mary, Pro Cathedral Parish (RC)**)

John Alexander (son):

Residence - 121 Lower Glouster Street - January 16, 1893

Catherin Henderson, daughter of Patrick Henderson & Ellen Swain

(daughter-in-law):

Residence - 121 Lower Glouster Street - January 16, 1893

  o Ellen Alexander – bapt. 1847 (Baptism, **St. Mary Parish (RC)**)

  o Mary Alexander – bapt. 1852 (Baptism, **St. Mary Parish (RC)**)

  o Matthew Alexander – bapt. 1855 (Baptism, **St. Mary Parish (RC)**)

  o Anne Alexander – bapt. 1860 (Baptism, **St. Mary Parish (RC)**)

Alexander Surname Ireland: 1600s to 1900s

- Matthew Alexander – bapt. 1862 (Baptism, **St. Mary Parish (RC)**)

Wedding Witnesses:

Matthew Donohoe & Mary Alexander

- John Alexander & Mary Malony – 25 Mar 1830 (Marriage, **St. Peter Parish**)
  - Mary Alexander – b. 12 Jan 1831, bapt. 2 Feb 1831 (Baptism, **Dunleckney Parish**)

John Alexander (father):

Residence - Bagenalstown, Dunleckney, Co. Carlow - March 25, 1830

Mary Malony (mother):

Residence - Upper Mount Street - February 2, 1831

- John Alexander & Mary Unknown
  - Catherine Alexander – bapt. 10 Jul 1735 (Baptism, **St. John Parish**)

- John Alexander & Mary Unknown
  - James Alexander – bapt. 8 Jun 1761 (Baptism, **St. Catherine Parish (RC)**)

- John Alexander & Mary Unknown
  - George Alexander – b. 10 May 1822, bapt. 26 May 1822 (Baptism, **St. Catherine Parish**)

- John Alexander & Mary Unknown
  - John Alexander – b. 1849, bapt. 1849 (Baptism, **St. Andrew Parish (RC)**)

- John Alexander & Mary Unknown
  - Anne Alexander & John O'Neill – 7 Sep 1865 (Marriage, **St. Nicholas Parish (RC)**)
    - John O'Neill – b. 26 Sep 1870, bapt. 10 Oct 1870 (Baptism, **St. Michan Parish (RC)**)

Hurst

Anne Alexander (daughter):

Residence - **23** Golden Lane - September **7, 1865**

John O'Neill, son of John O'Neill & Catherine Unknown (son-in-law):

Residence - **39** Golden Lane - September **7, 1865**

50 Beresford Street - October **10, 1870**

- John Alexander & Unknown
  - Catherine Alexander – bapt. 15 Oct 1648 (Baptism, **St. John Parish**)
  - John Alexander – bapt. 27 Dec 1650 (Baptism, **St. John Parish**)
  - Catherine Alexander – bapt. 6 Nov 1654 (Baptism, **St. John Parish**)
- John Alexander & Unknown
  - William Alexander – bapt. 20 Oct 1754 (Baptism, **St. Nicholas Within Parish**)
- John Alexander & Unknown
  - Elizabeth Alexander & Thomas Smyth – 31 Oct 1836 (Marriage, **St. Mary Parish (RC)**)
    - John Smyth – bapt. 1837 (Baptism, **St. Mary Parish (RC)**)

Wedding Witnesses:

John Alexander & William Whyte

- John Alexander & Unknown
  - John Alexander & Catherine Colleen – 28 Oct 1837 (Marriage, **St. Mary Parish (RC)**)
    - John Alexander – bapt. 1838 (Baptism, **St. Mary Parish (RC)**)
    - Michael Alexander – bapt. 1840 (Baptism, **St. Mary Parish (RC)**)
    - Stephen Alexander – bapt. 1843 (Baptism, **St. Mary Parish (RC)**)
    - Peter William Alexander – bapt. 1847 (Baptism, **St. Mary Parish (RC)**)

- Henry Alexander – bapt. 1849 (Baptism, **St. Mary Parish** (RC))

- Anne Alexander – bapt. 1851 (Baptism, **St. Mary Parish** (RC))

- George Alexander – bapt. 1854 (Baptism, **St. Mary Parish** (RC))

- Thomas Alexander – bapt. 1854 (Baptism, **St. Mary Parish** (RC))

- Mary Anne Alexander – bapt. 1857 (Baptism, **St. Mary Parish** (RC))

- Elizabeth Alexander – bapt. 1863 (Baptism, **St. Mary Parish** (RC))

Catherine Colleen, daughter of Owen Colleen (daughter-in-law).

Wedding Witnesses:

John Alexander & Owen Colleen

- John Alexander & Unknown
  - Arthur Alexander & Sarah Mary Johnston – 25 May 1857 (Marriage, **St. Thomas Parish**)

Signature:

Arthur Alexander (son):

Residence - 110 Lower Gardiner Street - May 25, 1857

Occupation - Solicitor - May 25, 1857

Sarah Mary Johnston, daughter of Arthur Johnston (daughter-in-law):

Residence - 112 Lower Gardiner Street - May 25, 1857

Relationship Status at Marriage - minor

Hurst

Arthur Johnston (father):

    Occupation - Medical Doctor

John Alexander (father):

    Occupation - Gentleman

Wedding Witnesses:

Coll Rochfort & Henry Concannon

Signatures:

- John Alexander & Unknown

Signature:

  o John Alexander & Caroline Jacob – 19 Apr 1866 (Marriage, St. Stephen Parish)

Signatures:

Alexander Surname Ireland: 1600s to 1900s

John Alexander (son):

    Residence - Callan, Co. Kilkenny - April 19, 1866

    Occupation - Clerk in Holy Orders - April 19, 1866

Caroline Jacob, daughter of John Edmund Jacob (daughter-in-law):

    Residence - 102 Lower Baggot Street - April 19, 1866

    Relationship at Marriage - minor

John Edmund Jacob (father):

    Occupation - Medical Doctor

John Alexander (father):

    Occupation - L. L. D. Clerk in Holy Orders

Wedding Witnesses:

Ar Jacob & Arthur C. Alexander

Signatures:

- John Alexander & Unknown
  - John Frederick Alexander, bur. 7 Aug 1894 (Burial, **George Parish**) & Augusta Anne McGuigan, b. 1847, bur. 10 Apr 1894 (Burial, **George Parish**) – 2 Jul 1867 (Marriage, **St. Mark Parish**)

Hurst

Signatures:

Signatures (Marriage):

- John Frederick Alexander, b. 27 Mar 1873, bapt. 25 Apr 1873 (Baptism, **St. Mark Parish**)

  & Ethel Margery Peel – 19 Jan 1900 (Marriage, **St. Paul Parish**)

Signatures:

- George Frederick Alexander – b. 14 Dec 1901, bapt. 29 Aug 1901 (Baptism, **St. James Parish**)

Alexander Surname Ireland: 1600s to 1900s

John Frederick Alexander (son):

    Residence - 4 Ellen Terrace, Auburn Street - January 19, 1900

        12 South View Terrace - August 29, 1901

    Occupation - Commercial Traveller - January 19, 1900

                        August 29, 1901

Ethel Margery Peel, daughter of Joseph Peel (daughter-in-law):

    Residence - 56 Queen Street - January 19, 1900

Joseph Peel (father):

Signature:

    Occupation - Wool Merchant

John Frederick Alexander (father):

    Occupation - Town Church Minister

Hurst

Wedding Witnesses:

Beatrice Mary Peel, George R. Grice, & Joseph Peel

Signatures:

- Augusta Margaret Alexander – b. 13 May 1876, bapt. 28 Jun 1876 (Baptism, **St. Mark Parish**), bur. 28 Feb 1877 (Burial, **George Parish**)

Augusta Margaret Alexander (deceased):

Residence - 135 Townsend Street - before February 28, 1877

Age at Death - 9 months

- Augusta Anne Alexander – b. 4 Oct 1878, bapt. 13 Nov 1878 (Baptism, **St. Mark Parish**)
- William John Alexander & Elizabeth Anne Sinnott Sherwood – 18 Sep 1893 (Marriage, **St. George Parish**)

Signatures:

Alexander Surname Ireland: 1600s to 1900s

William John Alexander (son):

    Residence - 4 Ellen Terrace - September 18, 1893

    Occupation - Clerk - September 18, 1893

Elizabeth Anne Sinnott Sherwood, daughter of Thomas Sinnott (daughter-in-law):

    Residence - 20 St. Catherine's Terrace - September 18, 1893

    Relationship Status at Marriage - widow

Thomas Sinnott (father):

    Occupation - Builder

John Frederick Alexander (father):

    Occupation - Clerk

Wedding Witnesses:

Henry Sinnott & John Frederick Alexander

Signatures:

John Frederick Alexander (son):

    Residence - 7 Townsend Street - July 2, 1867

        135 Townsend Street - April 25, 1873

        June 28, 1876

Hurst

November 13, 1878

4 Ellen Terrace - Before August 7, 1894

Occupation - Missionary - July 2, 1867

Scripture Reader - April 25, 1873

June 28, 1876

Jail Missionary of 26 M - November 13, 1878

Augusta Anne McGuigan, daughter of George McGuigan (daughter-in-law):

Residence - 12 D'Olier Street - July 2, 1867

4 Ellen Terrace - before April 10, 1894

Age at Death - 47 years

George McGuigan (father):

Signature:

Occupation - Missionary

John Alexander (father):

Occupation - Farmer

Wedding Witnesses:

Timothy Clesham & George McGuigan

Signatures:

- John Alexander & Unknown

  o Frances Alexander & Charles Henry Travers – 19 Oct 1847 (Marriage, **Cloydagh Parish**)

Signatures:

Frances Alexander (daughter):

Residence - Cloydagh - October 19, 1847

Charles Henry Travers, son of Thomas Otho Travers (son-in-law):

Residence - Cloydagh - October 19, 1847

Occupation - Clergyman - October 19, 1847

Thomas Otho Travers (father):

Occupation - Captain in the East India Company Service

Hurst

John Alexander (father):

    Occupation - Gentleman

Wedding Witnesses:

R. Otho Travers & Lorenzo William Alexander

Signatures:

- o Lorenzo William Alexander & Harriet Bruen – 25 Jun 1857 (Marriage, **Painestown Parish**)

Signature:

Signatures (Marriage):

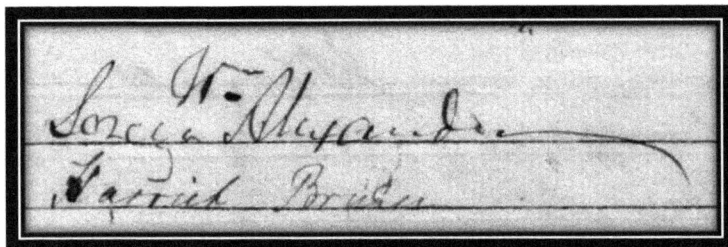

- Henry Bruen Alexander – b. 8 Nov 1860, bapt. 23 Dec 1860 (Baptism, **Painestown - St. Anne Parish**)

- Anne Cranston Alexander – b. 31 Jul 1862, bapt. 14 Sep 1862 (Baptism, **Painestown - St. Anne Parish**)

Lorenzo William Alexander (son):

Residence - Milford, Carlow - June 25, 1857

Straw Hall, Carlow - December 23, 1860

September 14, 1862

Occupation - Esquire - June 25, 1857

December 23, 1860

September 14, 1862

Harriet Bruen, daughter of Henry Bruen (daughter-in-law):

Residence - Oak Park, Carlow - June 25, 1857

Hurst

Henry Bruen (father):

Signatures:

Occupation - Esquire

John Alexander (father):

Occupation - Esquire

Wedding Witnesses:

Henry Bruen, Harriet Ruttledge, & Elizabeth Doyne

Signatures:

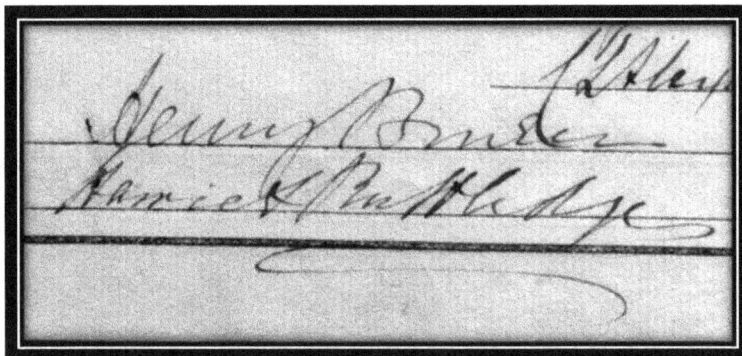

- John Alexander & Unknown

  - Robert Thomas Alexander & Elizabeth Brownrigg, b. 1850 – 25 Nov 1869 (Marriage, **Taney**

    Parish)

Signatures:

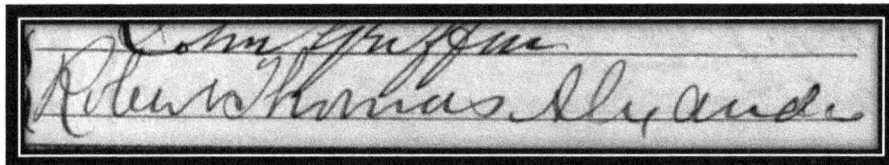

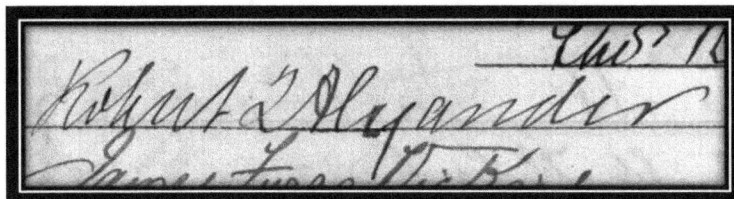

Hurst

- Jeanette Isabel Alexander & Sydney Furze Vickers – 1 Aug 1896 (Marriage, **Rathmines Parish**)

Signatures:

Jeanette Isabel Alexander (daughter):

　　Residence - 16 Palmerston Road - August 1, 1896

Sydney Furze Vickers, son of James Vickers (son-in-law):

　　Residence - 51 Lenham Gardens, London West - August 1, 1896

　　Occupation - Gentleman - August 1, 1896

James Furze Vickers (father):

Signature:

　　Occupation - Distiller

Robert Thomas Alexander (father):

　　Occupation - Merchant

Alexander Surname Ireland: 1600s to 1900s

Wedding Witnesses:

Robert Thomas Alexander & James Furze Vickers

Signatures:

- Robert Alexander & Julia Stynes – 30 Jun 1898 (Marriage, **Clondalkin Parish (RC)**)

Robert Alexander (son):

Residence - 60 Palmerstown Road - June 30, 1898

Julia Stynes, daughter of James Stynes & Catherine Callaghan (daughter-in-law):

Residence - Naas Road - June 30, 1898

Wedding Witnesses:

Patrick Stynes & Mary Stynes

Robert Thomas Alexander (son):

Residence - Somerstown, Cork - November 25, 1869

Occupation - Merchant - November 25, 1869

Elizabeth Brownrigg, daughter of William Henry Brownrigg (daughter-in-law):

Residence - Ross Hill, Milltown - November 25, 1869

Age at Marriage - 19 years

Hurst

William Henry Brownrigg (father):

   Occupation - Coal Proprietor

John Alexander (father):

   Occupation - Merchant

   o   Charles Alexander & Victoria Elizabeth Griffin – 26 Jun 1866 (Marriage, St. George

       Parish)

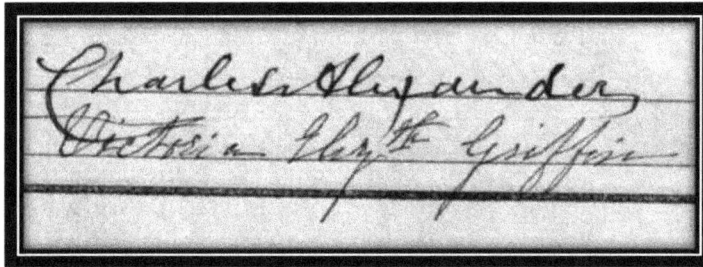

Signatures:

Charles Alexander (son):

   Residence - 7 Middle Gardiner Street - June 26, 1866

   Occupation - Seed Merchant - June 26, 1866

Victoria Elizabeth Griffin, daughter of John Griffin (daughter-in-law):

   Residence - 8 Summer Hill - June 26, 1866

   Relationship Status at Marriage - minor

John Griffin (father):

Signature:

    Occupation - Coal Merchant

John Alexander (father):

    Occupation - Seed Merchant

Wedding Witnesses:

John Griffin & Robert Thomas Alexander

Signatures:

Hurst

- John Alexander & Unknown

  o George Alexander, b. 1814, bur. 17 Nov 1893 (Burial, **Carlow Parish**) & Susan Henn
    Collins, b. 1833, bur. 2 Jul 1895 (Burial, **Carlow Parish**) – 28 Feb 1861 (Marriage, **St.
    Anne Parish**)

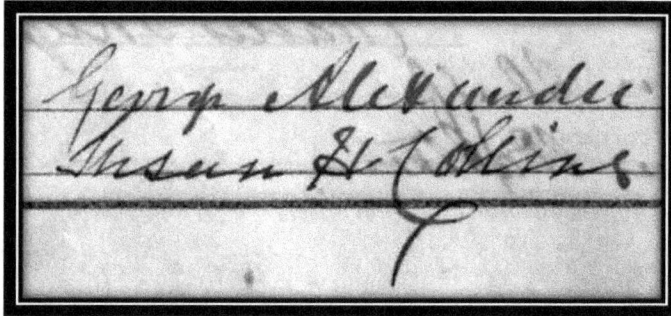

Signatures:

  ▪ Walter Lorenzo Alexander – b. 8 Sep 1872, bapt. 27 Oct 1872 (Baptism, **Wells Parish**)

George Alexander (son):

Residence - Saintfield, Co. Down - February 28, 1861

Rathvinden - October 27, 1872

Erindale, Carlow - before November 17, 1893

Occupation - Barrister at Law - February 28, 1861

Esquire - October 27, 1872

Before November 17, 1893

Age at Death - 79 years

Alexander Surname Ireland: 1600s to 1900s

Susan Henn Collins, daughter of Stephen Collins (daughter-in-law):

Residence - 13 Clare Street - February 28, 1861

171 Victoria Street, London - before July 2, 1895

Age at Death - 62 years

Stephen Collins (father):

Occupation - Q C Barrister at Law

John Alexander (father):

Occupation - Esquire

Wedding Witnesses:

J. Henn & John J. Stanford

Signatures:

- John Alexander & Unknown
  - Anne Alexander & Philip Cantlon – 30 Jul 1867 (Marriage, **Clonagoose Parish**)

Signatures:

Hurst

Anne Alexander (daughter):

    Residence - Ballytiglea - July 30, 1867

Philip Cantlon, son of John Cantlon (son-in-law):

    Residence - St. Mullins (Marley) - July 30, 1867

    Occupation - Farmer - July 30, 1867

John Cantlon (father):

    Occupation - Farmer

John Alexander (father):

    Occupation - Farmer

Wedding Witnesses:

John Bennett & Abraham Deacon

Signatures:

- Charles Alexander & Sophie Anne Bennett – 28 Jun 1883 (Marriage, **Clonagoose Parish**)

Signatures:

66

- Ellen Harriet Alexander – b. 3 Nov 1884, bapt. 16 Nov 1884 (Baptism, **Clonagoose Parish**)

- Annette Sophie Alexander – b. 26 Jun 1888, bapt. 16 Sep 1888 (Baptism, **Clonagoose Parish**)

- David Gibson Alexander – b. 31 Aug 1890, bapt. 26 Oct 1890 (Baptism, **Clonagoose Parish**)

- Isabel Margaret Alexander – b. 16 Sep 1891, bapt. 8 Nov 1891 (Baptism, **Clonagoose Parish**)

- John William Alexander – b. 14 Feb 1893, bapt. 14 Feb 1893 (Baptism, **Clonagoose Parish**)

- Eva Mary Alexander – b. 13 Jun 1894, bapt. 28 Jun 1894 (Baptism, **Clonagoose Parish**)

- Ada Teresa Alexander – b. 8 Nov 1895, bapt. 26 Dec 1895 (Baptism, **Clonagoose Parish**)

- Kathleen Sarah Alexander – b. 26 Feb 1897, bapt. 25 Apr 1897 (Baptism, **Clonagoose Parish**)

Charles Alexander (son):

Residence - Borris - June 28, 1883

November 16, 1884

Ballytiglea Borris - September 16, 1888

Ballytiglea - October 26, 1890

November 8, 1891

February 14, 1893

June 28, 1894

Hurst

December 26, 1895

April 25, 1897

Occupation - Sub Constable R. I. C. - June 28, 1883

Constable R. I. C. - November 16, 1884

September 16, 1888

Farmer - October 26, 1890

November 8, 1891

February 14, 1893

June 28, 1894

December 26, 1895

April 25, 1897

Sophie Anne Bennett, daughter of John Bennett (daughter-in-law):

Residence - Borris - June 28, 1883

John Bennett (father):

Signature:

Occupation - Farmer

John Alexander (father):

Occupation - Farmer

Alexander Surname Ireland: 1600s to 1900s

Wedding Witnesses:

William H. Bennett & Harriet M. Bennett

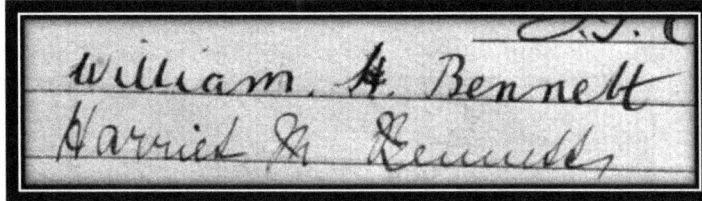

Signatures:

- John Gavan Alexander & Agnes McLean Alexander

  - Agnes Alexander – b. 15 Oct 1891, bapt. 3 Nov 1892 (Baptism, **North Strand Parish**)

  - Donald Graham Alexander – b. 16 May 1894, bapt. 1 Jun 1894 (Baptism, **St. Mary Parish**)

  - Agnes McLean Alexander – b. 22 Sep 1896, bapt. 31 Dec 1896 (Baptism, **North Strand Parish**)

  - Hector McDonald Alexander – b. 4 May 1900, bapt. 31 May 1900 (Baptism, **North Strand Parish**)

John Alexander (father):

Residence - 2 Gaelic Street - November 3, 1892

3 Julian Place - June 1, 1894

5 Newcomen Avenue - December 31, 1896

3 Newcomen Court - May 31, 1900

Occupation - Engineer - November 3, 1892

Engine Driver - June 1, 1894

December 31, 1896

Hurst

May 31, 1900

- John Henry Alexander & Unknown

  - Walter Henry Alexander & Margaret Fitzgerald – 6 Aug 1888 (Marriage, **St. Peter Parish**)

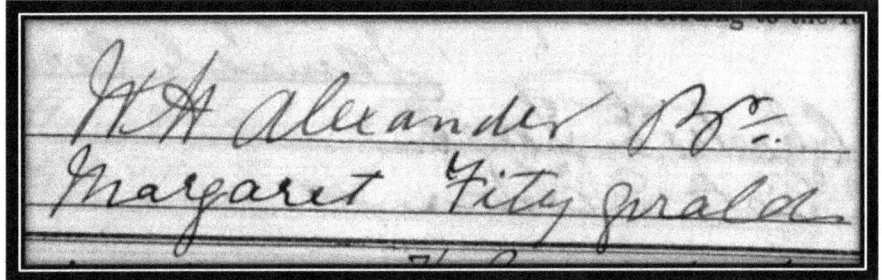

Signatures:

- Charles Henry Alexander – b. 8 Jul 1889, bapt. 4 Aug 1889 (Baptism, **Portobello Barracks Parish**)

Walter Henry Alexander (son):

Residence - Portobello Barracks - August 6, 1888

7 Grove Road, Portobello - August 4, 1889

Occupation - Bombardier Royal Horse Artillery - August 6, 1888

August 4, 1889

Margaret Fitzgerald, daughter of James Fitzgerald (daughter-in-law):

Residence - Portobello Barracks - August 6, 1888

James Fitzgerald (father):

Occupation - Soldier

John Henry Alexander (father):

Occupation - Professor of Music

Wedding Witnesses:

Edward Stocker & Mary Paterson

Signatures:

- Jonathan Alexander & Unknown

  o William Alexander & Ellen Sheridan – 13 Aug 1867 (Marriage, **Tralee Parish**)

Signatures:

  ▪ John Alexander – b. 22 Jun 1868, bapt. 24 Jun 1868 (Baptism, **Tralee Parish (RC)**)

William Alexander (son):

Residence - Tralee Barracks - August 13, 1867

Tralee - June 24, 1868

Occupation - Private, Soldier - August 13, 1867

Hurst

Ellen Sheridan, daughter of Thomas Sheridan (daughter-in-law):

    Residence - Tralee - August 13, 1867

    Occupation - Dress Maker - August 13, 1867

    Relationship Status at Marriage - minor age

Thomas Sheridan (father):

    Occupation - Engineer

Jonathan Alexander (father):

    Occupation - Silver Smith

Wedding Witnesses:

Richard Frycon & Frank Verso

Signatures:

- Joseph Alexander & Catherine White

  - Mary Anne Alexander – bapt. Dec 1827 (Baptism, **St. Catherine Parish (RC)**)

- Joseph Alexander & Margaret Unknown

  - Joseph Alexander – bapt. 18 Mar 1824 (Baptism, **St. Nicholas Parish (RC)**)

- Joseph Alexander & Margaret White

  - Robert Joseph Alexander – bapt. 1832 (Baptism, **St. Nicholas Parish (RC)**)

  - James Alexander – bapt. 28 Sep 1832 (Baptism, **St. Catherine Parish (RC)**)

Alexander Surname Ireland: 1600s to 1900s

- o Thomas Alexander – bapt. 1 Nov 1835 (Baptism, **St. Catherine Parish** (RC))

- o Robert Alexander – bapt. 6 Jul 1838 (Baptism, **St. Catherine Parish** (RC))

- o Margaret Julia Alexander – bapt. Mar 1841 (Baptism, **St. Catherine Parish** (RC))

- o Francis Patrick Alexander – bapt. 10 Dec 1844 (Baptism, **St. Catherine Parish** (RC))

- Joseph Alexander & Mary Alexander

  - o Ellen Alexander – bapt. 5 Nov 1831 (Baptism, **St. Mary, Pro Cathedral Parish** (RC))

- Joseph Alexander & Mary Bigford

  - o Joseph Alexander – bapt. 5 Jun 1850 (Baptism, **St. Michan Parish** (RC))

- Joseph Alexander & Mary Callender

  - o Mary Alexander – bapt. 26 Aug 1844 (Baptism, **St. Nicholas Parish** (RC))

- Joseph Alexander & Mary Cansler

  - o Eleanor Alexander – bapt. 12 Jan 1847 (Baptism, **St. Catherine Parish** (RC))

  - o Thomas Alexander – bapt. 3 Oct 1848 (Baptism, **St. Catherine Parish** (RC))

- Joseph Alexander & Mary Unknown

  - o Thomas Alexander & Mary Anne Fox – 5 Apr 1875 (Marriage, **St. Catherine Parish** (RC))

    - Mary Ellen Alexander – b. 23 Jun 1876, bapt. 30 Jun 1876 (Baptism, **St. Nicholas Parish** (RC))

    - Jane Alexander – b. 2 Jun 1878, bapt. 3 Jun 1878 (Baptism, **St. Nicholas Parish** (RC))

    - Thomas Alexander – b. 10 Feb 1880, bapt. 13 Feb 1880 (Baptism, **St. Audoen Parish** (RC))

    - Christine Alexander – b. 3 Jan 1883, bapt. 5 Jan 1883 (Baptism, **St. Audoen Parish** (RC))

    - Margaret Frances Alexander – b. 16 Jul 1887, Bapt. 19 Jul 1887 (Baptism, **St. Audoen Parish** (RC))

Hurst

Thomas Alexander (son):

Residence - 22 Black Hall Row - April 5, 1875

134 Francis Street - June 30, 1876

102 Francis Street - June 3, 1878

35 High Street - February 13, 1880

January 5, 1883

July 19, 1887

Mary Anne Fox, daughter of Thomas Fox & Bridget Unknown (daughter-in-law):

Residence - 5 Wormwood Gate - April 5, 1875

- Joseph Alexander & Mary Anne Samuel – 13 Nov 1826 (Marriage, St. Mary, Haddington Road Parish (RC))
  - o James Alexander – bapt. 1836 (Baptism, St. Mary Parish (RC))
  - o Thomas Alexander – bapt. 1838 (Baptism, St. Mary Parish (RC))
  - o John Alexander – bapt. 1839 (Baptism, St. Mary Parish (RC))
  - o Margaret Alexander – bapt. 1842 (Baptism, St. Mary Parish (RC))
- Joseph Alexander & Mary Anne Unknown
  - o Mary Anne Alexander – bapt. 1829 (Baptism, St. Andrew Parish (RC))
- Joseph Alexander & Mary S. Bridges – 12 Sep 1831 (Marriage, St. John Parish)
- Joseph Alexander & Unknown
  - o Thomas Alexander & Winifred Leary – 2 Jul 1865 (Marriage, St. Andrew Parish (RC))

Alexander Surname Ireland: 1600s to 1900s

Thomas Alexander (son):

    Residence - 12 Clarendon Street - July 2, 1865

Winifred Leary, daughter of Michael Leary (daughter-in-law):

    Residence - 12 Clarendon Street - July 2, 1865

- Joseph Alexander & Unknown
  - Joseph Alexander & Frances Ada Hamilton – 13 Sep 1865 (Marriage, **St. George Parish**)

Signatures:

Joseph Alexander (son):

    Residence - 10 Gardiner's Place & Five Mile Town, Co. Tyrone -

                                   September 13, 1865

    Occupation - Solicitor - September 13, 1865

Frances Ada Hamilton, daughter of John Hamilton (daughter-in-law):

    Residence -Drumaconner House, Parish of Kilmore, Co. Monaghan -

                                   September 13, 1865

John Hamilton (father):

    Occupation - Esquire

Hurst

Joseph Alexander (father):

Occupation - Merchant

Wedding Witnesses:

John Fawcett & J. Teevan

Signatures:

- Joseph Alexander & Unknown
  - Francis Alexander & Sarah Deakes – 31 Mar 1874 (Marriage, **St. Nicholas Parish** (RC))
    - Joseph Alexander – b. 1869, bapt. 1869 (Baptism, **St. Andrew Parish** (RC))
    - Mary Anne Alexander – b. 20 Jan 1871, bapt. 30 Jan 1871 (Baptism, **St. Nicholas Parish** (RC))
    - Francis Michael Alexander – b. 24 Sep 1872, bapt. 30 Sep 1872 (Baptism, **St. Nicholas Parish** (RC))
    - Matthew J. Alexander – b. 1 Nov 1874, bapt. 9 Nov 1874 (Baptism, **St. Nicholas Parish** (RC))
    - Sarah Alexander – b. 19 Feb 1876, bapt. 28 Feb 1876 (Baptism, **St. Nicholas Parish** (RC))
    - Elizabeth Anne Alexander – b. 19 Oct 1880, bapt. 29 Oct 1880 (Baptism, **St. Nicholas Parish** (RC))

Alexander Surname Ireland: 1600s to 1900s

Francis Alexander (son):

Residence - 33 Temple Bar - 1869

35 New Market - January 30, 1871

1 Mill Lane - September 30, 1872

2 Mill Lane - March 31, 1874

November 9, 1874

5 Ward's Hill - February 28, 1876

October 29, 1880

Sarah Deakes, daughter of Nicholas Deakes (daughter-in-law):

Residence - 2 Mill Lane - March 31, 1874

- Joseph Alexander Alexander & Mary Unknown

  o Joseph Alexander – bapt. Nov 1851 (Baptism, **SS. Michael & John Parish (RC)**)

- Matthew Alexander & Margaret Mary Unknown

  o Mary Alexander – bapt. 12 May 1776 (Baptism, **St. Paul Parish**)

  o George Alexander – bapt. 11 Apr 1778 (Baptism, **St. Paul Parish**)

  o Mary Alexander – bapt. 14 Feb 1779 (Baptism, **St. Paul Parish**)

  o Elizabeth Alexander – bapt. 3 Jun 1780 (Baptism, **St. Paul Parish**)

- Matthew Alexander & Margaret Elizabeth Alexander

  o James Alexander – bapt. 7 Jul 1782 (Baptism, **St. Paul Parish**)

  o Richard Alexander – bapt. 28 Dec 1783 (Baptism, **St. Paul Parish**)

  o John Alexander – bapt. 27 Aug 1785 (Baptism, **St. Paul Parish**)

Hurst

- Michael Alexander & Elizabeth Sarah Downey – 30 Sep 1842 (Marriage, **St. Mary Parish** (RC))

  o Christopher Alexander – bapt. 1843 (Baptism, **St. Mary Parish** (RC))

  o John Alexander – bapt. 1847 (Baptism, **St. Mary Parish** (RC))

  o Joseph Alexander – bapt. 1848 (Baptism, **St. Mary Parish** (RC))

  o Anne Alexander – bapt. 1852 (Baptism, **St. Mary Parish** (RC))

  o Sarah Mary Alexander – bapt. 1854 (Baptism, **St. Mary Parish** (RC))

  o Mary Alexander – bapt. 1859 (Baptism, **St. Mary Parish** (RC))

  o James Alexander – bapt. 1861 (Baptism, **St. Mary Parish** (RC))

Wedding Witnesses:

John Alexander & Sarah Colleen

- Moses Alexander & Margaret McDonnell – 5 Dec 1762 (Marriage, **St. Mary Parish**)

  o Frances Alexander – bapt. 3 Jan 1774 (Baptism, **St. Mary Parish**)

Moses Alexander (father):

Residence - Mary's Abby - January 3, 1774

- Nathaniel Alexander & Florinda Unknown

  o Robert Jackson Alexander – b. 18 Jan 1843, bapt. 21 Feb 1843 (Baptism, **St. Peter Parish**)

Nathaniel Alexander (father):

Residence - 1 Fitzwilliam Place, Portagemore House - February 21, 1843

Occupation - Gentleman - February 21, 1843

- Newberry Alexander & Catherine Margaret Alexander

  o Mary Alexander – bapt. 12 Dec 1736 (Baptism, **St. Mark Parish**)

Alexander Surname Ireland: 1600s to 1900s

- o   Catherine Alexander – bapt. 4 May 1740 (Baptism, **St. Mark Parish**)

Newberry Alexander (father):

Residence - Lazer's Hill - May 4, 1740

- Patrick Alexander & Eleanor Walsh – 9 Aug 1796 (Marriage, **St. Nicholas Parish (RC)**)

Wedding Witnesses:

John Alexander & Peter Fannan

- Patrick Alexander & Mary Byrne (B y r n e) – 6 Nov 1845 (Marriage, **SS. Michael & John Parish (RC)**)

Wedding Witnesses:

John Byrne & Anne Ward

- Patrick Alexander & Mary Mallin – 16 Sep 1762 (Marriage, **St. Catherine Parish (RC)**)
  - o   Elizabeth Alexander – b. 1766, bapt. 1766 (Baptism, **St. Catherine Parish (RC)**)
  - o   George Alexander – bapt. 16 Jul 1770 (Baptism, **St. Catherine Parish (RC)**)
- Peter Alexander & Hannah Evelyn Alexander
  - o   Peter Fraser Alexander – b. 10 Jun 1894, bapt. 25 Jun 1894 (Baptism, **Arbour Hill Barracks Parish**)

Peter Alexander (father):

Residence - Arbour Hill Medical Quarters - June 25, 1894

Occupation - Color Sergeant 2nd Gordon highlanders - June 25, 1894

Hurst

- Reuben Alexander & Mary Elizabeth Alexander

  - Gertrude Mary Alexander – b. 9 Jul 1864, bapt. 25 Jan 1885 (Baptism, **Rathmines Parish**)

Reuben Alexander (father):

Residence - 4 Maxwell Road - January 25, 1885

Occupation - Merchant - January 25, 1885

- Robert Alexander & Eleanor Cullen – 25 Oct 1826 (Marriage, **St. Paul Parish**)

  - Joseph Alexander – bapt. 31 Dec 1827 (Baptism, **Rathmines Parish (RC)**)

  - Mary Alexander – bapt. 14 Jul 1829 (Baptism, **SS. Michael & John Parish (RC)**)

  - Hugh Alexander – bapt. 1 Jul 1830 (Baptism, **SS. Michael & John Parish (RC)**)

  - Alice Alexander – bapt. 4 Aug 1831 (Baptism, **SS. Michael & John Parish (RC)**)

  - Robert Alexander – bapt. 1 Jun 1834 (Baptism, **Rathmines Parish (RC)**)

  - Michael Alexander – bapt. 20 May 1836 (Baptism, **Rathmines Parish (RC)**)

- Robert Alexander & Jane Moran – 16 Feb 1858 (Marriage, **St. Andrew Parish (RC)**)

  - Joseph Alexander, b. 1858, bapt. 1858 (Baptism, **St. Andrew Parish (RC)**) & Julia Hayden

    – 14 Nov 1890 (Marriage, **St. Mary, Pro Cathedral Parish (RC)**)

    - Jane Christine Alexander – b. 1 Jun 1893, bapt. 5 Jun 1893 (Baptism, **St. Mary, Pro**

      Cathedral Parish (RC))

    - Robert Joseph Alexander – b. 1895, bapt. 1895 (Baptism, **St. Andrew Parish (RC)**)

Joseph Alexander (son):

Residence - 41 Marlborough Street - November 14, 1890

40 Summer Hill - June 5, 1893

27 King Street - 1895

Alexander Surname Ireland: 1600s to 1900s

Julia Hayden, daughter of Patrick Hayden & Jane Murray (daughter-in-law):

Residence - 41 Marlborough Street - November 14, 1890

- o John Alexander – b. 1859, bapt. 1859 (Baptism, **St. Andrew Parish (RC)**)

- o Mary Anne Alexander – b. 1861, bapt. 1861 (Baptism, **St. Andrew Parish (RC)**)

- o Margaret Jane Alexander – b. 1864, bapt. 1864 (Baptism, **St. Andrew Parish (RC)**)

- o Robert Alexander – b. 1865, bapt. 1865 (Baptism, **St. Andrew Parish (RC)**)

Robert Alexander (father):

Residence - 7 Fade Street - 1858

5 Fade Street - 1859

6 Fade Street - 1861

54 Lower Stephen's Street - 1864

47 Stephen Street - 1864

- • Robert Alexander, bur. 28 Dec 1682 (Burial, **St. Michan Parish**) & Jane Unknown

  - o Cornelia (C o r n e l i a) Alexander – bapt. 5 Dec 1675 (Baptism, **St. Michan Parish**), bur. 26 Oct 1677 (Burial, **St. Michan Parish**)

  - o Cornelia (C o r n e l i a) Alexander – bur. 12 May 1678 (Burial, **St. Michan Parish**)

  - o Jane Alexander – bapt. 11 Jul 1679 (Baptism, **St. Michan Parish**), bur. 7 Jul 1682 (Burial, **St. Michan Parish**)

Robert Alexander (father):

Occupation - Merchant - December 5, 1675

October 26, 1677

Hurst

May 12, 1678

July 7, 1682

December 28, 1682

Gentleman - July 11, 1679

- Robert Alexander & Margaret Alexander

  o Mathias Alexander – bapt. 18 Sep 1748 (Baptism, **St. Mark Parish**)

Robert Alexander (father):

Residence - Hawkin's Quay - September 18, 1748

- Robert Alexander & Mary Alexander

  o Robert Alexander – bapt. 29 Apr 1733 (Baptism, **St. Mark Parish**)

- Robert Alexander & Mary Forfor – 26 Dec 1721 (Burial, **St. Paul Parish**)

- Robert Alexander & Rose Brown

  o Robert Alexander – bapt. Jul 1827 (Baptism, **SS. Michael & John Parish (RC)**)

- Robert Alexander & Unknown

  o Robert Alexander & Louisa Isabel Bagley Armstrong (A r m s t r o n g) – 17 Feb 1863

    (Marriage, **St. Peter Parish**)

Signatures:

Alexander Surname Ireland: 1600s to 1900s

Robert Alexander (son):

> Residence - Glenmore, Millifont Parish, Drogheda - February 17, 1863

> Occupation - Esquire in the Indian Civil Service - February 17, 1863

Louisa Isabel Bagley Armstrong, daughter of Richard Bagley (daughter-in-law):

> Residence - 15 Leeson Park - February 17, 1863

> Relationship Status at Marriage - widow

Richard Bagley (father):

> Occupation - Officer in the Army

Robert Alexander (father):

> Occupation - Clergyman

Wedding Witnesses:

G. Nicholson & W. W. Bagley

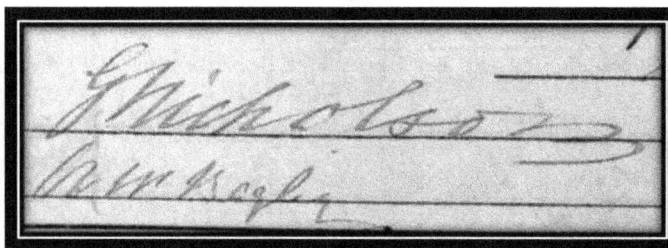

Signatures:

- Samuel Alexander & Sarah Harold – 11 Mar 1730 (Marriage, **Dingle Parish**)

Samuel Alexander (husband):

> Occupation - Captain in Stisted's Company - March 11, 1730

Hurst

Sarah Harold (wife):

Residence - Dingle - March 11, 1730

- Samuel Alexander & Unknown
  - John Adam Alexander & Edith Margaret Reeves – 15 Dec 1875 (Marriage, **St. Stephen Parish**)

Signatures:

John Adam Alexander (son):

Residence - 29 South Frederick Street - December 15, 1875

Occupation - Esquire C E - December 15, 1875

Edith Margaret Reeves, daughter of Edward Reeves (daughter-in-law):

Residence - 7 Lower Fitzwilliam Street - December 15, 1875

Edward Reeves (father):

Occupation - Solicitor

Samuel Alexander (father):

Occupation - Clerk in Holy Orders

Alexander Surname Ireland: 1600s to 1900s

Wedding Witnesses:

Charles M. Alexander & Richard S. Reeves

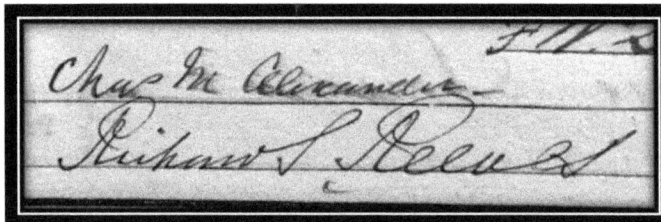

Signatures:

- Thomas Alexander & Alice Alexander

  o Eileen Alicia Alexander – b. 20 Aug 1899, bapt. 3 Sep 1899 (Baptism, **St. George Parish**)

Thomas Alexander (father):

Residence - 28 St. Ignatius Road - September 3, 1899

Occupation - Prison Warden - September 3, 1899

- Thomas Alexander & Eleanor Unknown

  o Eleanor Alexander – bapt. 5 Oct 1769 (Baptism, **St. Catherine Parish**)

Thomas Alexander (father):

Residence - Cork Street - October 5, 1769

- Thomas Alexander & Elizabeth Hickey

  o Peter Alexander – b. 5 Jun 1810, bapt. 12 Jun 1810 (Baptism, **St. Catherine Parish (RC)**)

  o Alice Alexander – bapt. 30 Jun 1816 (Baptism, **St. Nicholas Parish (RC)**)

Hurst

- Thomas Alexander & Jane Alexander
  - Ellen Jane Alexander – b. 24 Apr 1858, bapt. 2 May 1858 (Baptism, **St. Paul Parish**)

Thomas Alexander (father):

Residence - 9 Hendrick Street - May 2, 1858

Occupation - Policeman - May 2, 1858

- Thomas Alexander & Jane Haigh – 15 Feb 1836 (Marriage, **St. Peter Parish**)

Thomas Alexander (husband):

Residence - Buncrana, Lower Fagan, Co. Donegal - February 15, 1836

Jane Haigh (wife):

Residence - Harcourt Street, St. Peter Parish - February 15, 1836

- Thomas Alexander & Jane Unknown
  - Anne Alexander – bapt. 15 Sep 1733 (Baptism, **St. Nicholas Without Parish**)

Thomas Alexander (father):

Residence - Francis Street - September 15, 1733

- Thomas Alexander & Mary Alexander
  - Lucinda Ellen Alexander – b. 25 Jul 1862, bapt. 12 Aug 1862 (Baptism, **Clontarf Parish**)
  - Jeanette Louisa Alexander – b. 25 Jul 1862, bapt. 12 Aug 1862 (Baptism, **Clontarf Parish**)

Thomas Alexander (father):

Residence - Killester - August 12, 1862

Occupation - Medical Doctor - August 12, 1862

Alexander Surname Ireland: 1600s to 1900s

- Thomas Alexander & Mary Ardagh

  - Joseph Alexander – b. 1766, bapt. 1766 (Baptism, **St. Catherine Parish** (RC))

  - Anne Alexander – bapt. 21 Feb 1769 (Baptism, **St. Catherine Parish** (RC))

  - Thomas Alexander – bapt. 3 Dec 1775 (Baptism, **St. Catherine Parish** (RC))

  - Peter Alexander – bapt. 27 Jun 1779 (Baptism, **St. Catherine Parish** (RC))

  - James Alexander – bapt. 27 Jun 1782 (Baptism, **St. Catherine Parish** (RC))

- Thomas Alexander & Mary Early

  - Edward Alexander – b. 15 Dec 1868, bapt. 30 Dec 1868 (Baptism, **St. Michan Parish** (RC))

Thomas Alexander (father):

Residence - 72 Upper Dominick Street - December 30, 1868

- Thomas Alexander & Mary Unknown

  - Margaret Alexander – bapt. 19 Feb 1786 (Baptism, **St. Nicholas Parish** (RC))

- Thomas Alexander & Sarah Alexander, bur. 21 Jul 1780 (Burial, **St. Luke Parish**)

  - Jane Alexander – bapt. 22 Nov 1761 (Baptism, **St. Luke Parish**)

Sarah Alexander (mother):

Residence - House of Industry - before July 21, 1780

Cause of Death - old age

- Thomas Alexander & Sarah Unknown

  - John Alexander – bapt. 12 Apr 1764 (Baptism, **St. Catherine Parish**)

- Thomas Alexander & Unknown

    o Alexander Leech & Mary Bennett – 16 Oct 1849 (Marriage, **St. Catherine Parish**)

Signatures:

Alexander Leech (step-son):

    Residence - Portland Street - October 16, 1849

    Occupation - Servant - October 16, 1849

Mary Bennett, daughter of Thomas Bennett (daughter-in-law):

    Residence - Portland Street - October 16, 1849

Thomas Bennett (father):

    Occupation - Boot Maker

Thomas Alexander (father):

    Occupation - Servant

Alexander Surname Ireland: 1600s to 1900s

Wedding Witnesses:

Thomas Bennett & Winifred Watts

Signatures:

- Thomas Alexander & Unknown

  o William Alexander & Frances Geraldine Armstrong (A r m s t r o n g) – 15 Jan 1856 (Marriage,

  St. Mary Parish)

Signatures:

  ▪ Thomas Guy Alexander – b. 20 Jul 1857, bapt. 25 Oct 1857 (Baptism, **Rathmines Parish**)

  ▪ William Alexander – b. 7 Nov 1859, bapt. 18 Dec 1859 (Baptism, **Rathmines Parish**)

  ▪ Catherine Alexander – b. 18 Jun 1861, bapt. 21 Jul 1861 (Baptism, **Rathmines Parish**)

  ▪ Alfred Edward Alexander, b. 31 Jul 1863, bapt. 6 Sep 1863 (Baptism, **Sandford Parish**)

   (Baptism, **St. Peter Parish**) & Juliana Mary Waterson

Signature:

Hurst

- Frances Eileen Alexander – b. 29 Oct 1898, bapt. 28 Dec 1898 (Baptism, **St. Mathias Parish**)

- Frances Marion Alexander – b. 29 Oct 1898, bapt. 18 Nov 1898 (Baptism, **Rathmines Parish** (RC))

Alfred Edward Alexander (son):

Residence - 53B Rathmines Road - November 18, 1898

December 28, 1898

Occupation - Civil Service Clerk - December 28, 1898

- Frances Anne Alexander, b. 21 Apr 1865, bapt. 25 May 1865 (Baptism, **Sandford Parish**) (Baptism, **St. Peter Parish**) & Herbert Barnes (B a r n e s) – 11 Oct 1890 (Marriage, **Rathmines Parish** (RC))

Frances Anne Alexander (daughter):

Residence - 53 Rathmines Road - October 11, 1890

Herbert Barnes, son of Mark Barnes & Elizabeth Graham (son-in-law):

Residence - 4 Clare Terrace Street, Canal - October 11, 1890

Wedding Witnesses:

John A. O'Connell & Anne Barnes

- John Armstrong (A r m s t r o n g) Alexander – b. 26 Feb 1868, bapt. 10 Mar 1868 (Baptism, **St. Peter Parish**)

Alexander Surname Ireland: 1600s to 1900s

William Alexander (son):

    Residence - 75 South George's Street - January 15, 1856

        139 Rathmines - October 25, 1857

        December 18, 1859

        53 Rathmines Road - July 21, 1861

        Rathmines Road - September 6, 1863

        May 25, 1865

        53B Rathmines Road - May 25, 1865

        Rathmines - March 10, 1868

    Occupation - Draper - January 15, 1856

        October 25, 1857

        December 18, 1859

        July 21, 1861

        September 6, 1863

        Shopkeeper - May 25, 1865

        March 10, 1868

Frances Geraldine Armstrong, daughter of Thomas Armstrong

(daughter-in-law):

    Residence - 4 Henry Street - January 15, 1856

Thomas Armstrong (father):

Occupation - Officer in the 4th Dragoon Guards

Thomas Alexander (father):

Occupation - Gentleman

Wedding Witnesses:

Thomas Bowles & John Williams

Signatures:

- Thomas Alexander & Unknown

Signature:

 o Martha Todd Alexander & Henry Osborne (O s b o r n e) – 1 Oct 1862 (Marriage, **St. Thomas Parish**)

Signatures:

Alexander Surname Ireland: 1600s to 1900s

Martha Todd Alexander (daughter):

    Residence - 1 North Street - October 1, 1862

Henry Osborne, son of James Osborne (son-in-law):

    Residence - Hollywood, Co. Down - October 1, 1862

    Occupation - Clergyman - October 1, 1862

James Osborne (father):

    Occupation - Gentleman

Thomas Alexander (father):

    Occupation - Merchant

Wedding Witnesses:

Alexander Thomson Osborne & William Woods

Signatures:

Hurst

○ James Alexander & Jane Walmsley – 6 Sep 1871 (Marriage, **St. Anne Parish**)

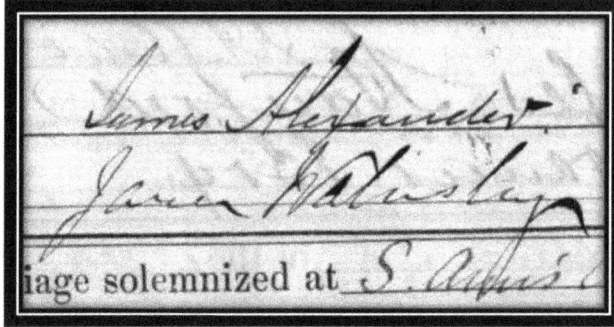

Signatures:

James Alexander (son):

    Residence - Kitteel, Co. Down - September 6, 1871

    Occupation - Manager of Bank - September 6, 1871

Jane Walmsley, daughter of James Walmsley (daughter-in-law):

    Residence - 18 South Frederick Street - September 6, 1871

James Walmsley (father):

Signature:

    Occupation - Gentleman

Thomas Alexander (father):

    Occupation - Merchant

Alexander Surname Ireland: 1600s to 1900s

Wedding Witnesses:

James Walmsley & Thomas Alexander

Signatures:

- o Thomas John Alexander & Ellen Irwin – 26 Jun 1879 (Marriage, **St. Thomas Parish**)

Signatures:

- ▪ William Nicholas Alexander – b. 11 Sep 1880, bapt. 8 Oct 1880 (Baptism, **Harold's Cross**

  Parish)

- ▪ Thomas Irwin Alexander – b. 24 Feb 1882, bapt. 17 Mar 1882 (Baptism, **Harold's Cross**

  Parish)

Thomas John Alexander (son):

Residence - 141 Belfield Terrace - June 26, 1879

No. 141 Rathmines - October 8, 1880

Omagh, Co. Tyrone - March 17, 1882

Occupation - School Inspector - June 26, 1879

Inspector of Schools - October 8, 1880

Hurst

Inspector National Boys Schools - March 17, 1882

Ellen Irwin, daughter of William Irwin (daughter-in-law):

Residence - Custom House - June 26, 1879

Relationship Status at Marriage - minor

William Irwin (father):

Occupation - Clergyman

Thomas Alexander (father):

Occupation - Store Keeper

Wedding Witnesses:

Robert W. Couser & Mary Jane Bailey

Signatures:

- Thomas Alexander & Winifred Scully
  - Margaret Mary Alexander – b. 2 Feb 1870, bapt. 11 Feb 1870 (Baptism, St. Nicholas Parish (RC))
  - Thomas Alexander – b. 12 Oct 1871, bapt. 24 Oct 1871 (Baptism, St. Catherine Parish (RC))

Alexander Surname Ireland: 1600s to 1900s

- o Robert Patrick Alexander – b. 24 Mar 1873, bapt. 31 Mar 1873 (Baptism, **St. Nicholas Parish (RC)**)

- o Mary Anne Alexander – b. 24 Jan 1875, bapt. 26 Jan 1875 (Baptism, **St. Catherine Parish (RC)**)

- o Nicholas Alexander – b. 6 Feb 1877, bapt. Feb 1877 (Baptism, **St. Catherine Parish (RC)**)

Thomas Alexander (father):

Residence - 4 Ne Market - February 11, 1870

21 Chamber Street - October 24, 1871

5 New Market - March 31, 1873

18 Chamber Street - January 26, 1875

February 1877

- • Thomas Naritt Alexander & Unknown

Signatures:

Hurst

- o Elizabeth Anne Alexander & Carlyle Woodhouse Williams – 17 Feb 1897 (Marriage, **St. Paul Parish**)

Signature:

Signatures (Marriage):

Elizabeth Anne Alexander (daughter):

Residence - 15 Aberdeen Street, Infirmary Road, Dublin - February 17, 1897

Carlyle Woodhouse Williams, son of John Williams (son-in-law):

Residence - 7 Munster Street, Dublin - February 17, 1897

Occupation - Civil Service Clerk - February 17, 1897

John Williams (father):

Occupation - Post Master

Thomas Naritt Alexander (father):

Occupation - R I C

Wedding Witnesses:

James Williams & Thomas Naritt Alexander

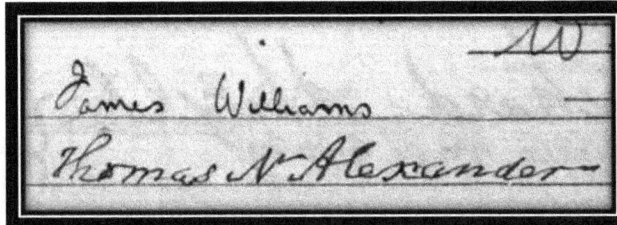

Signatures:

- Unknown Alexander & Alberta Alexander

    o Julia Alexander – b. 1 Jan 1894, bapt. 3 Jan 1894 (Baptism, **St. Mary, Pro Cathedral Parish (RC)**)

Alberta Alexander (mother):

Residence - 17 Lower Gardiner Street - January 3, 1894

- Unknown Alexander & Elizabeth Alexander

    o Joan Alexander – bapt. 14 Apr 1672 (Baptism, **St. Audoen Parish**), bur. 22 Dec 1672 (Burial, **St. Audoen Parish**)

- Unknown Alexander & Emily Alexander

    o Thomas Alexander – b. 21 Feb 1893, bapt. 28 Feb 1893 (Baptism, **Rotunda Chapel Parish**)

Emily Alexander (mother):

Residence - 24 North Cumberland Street - February 28, 1893

Occupation - Domestic Servant - February 28, 1893

Hurst

- Unknown Alexander & Emily Keating (1st Marriage)

- Emily Keating Alexander (2nd Marriage) & William Hawthorn (H a w t h o r n) – 3 Dec 1891 (Marriage, St. Thomas Parish)

Signatures:

Emily Keating Alexander, daughter of James Keating (wife) (2nd Marriage):

Residence - 44 Marlborough Street - December 3, 1891

Relationship Status at Marriage - widow

William Hawthorn, son of William Hawthorn (husband):

Residence - 44 Marlborough Street - December 3, 1891

Occupation - Book Binder - December 3, 1891

Relationship Status at Marriage - widow

William Hawthorn (father):

Occupation - Marble Cutter

James Keating (father):

Occupation - Gentleman Farmer

Alexander Surname Ireland: 1600s to 1900s

Wedding Witnesses:

Charles Finucane & Margaret Bergin

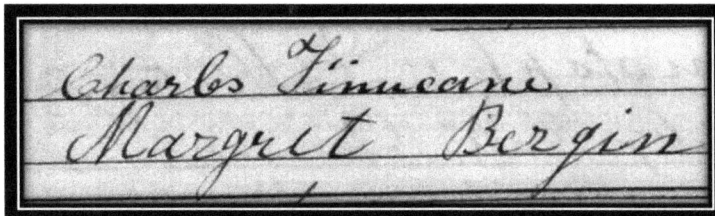

Signatures:

- Unknown Alexander & Margaret Unknown

  o Robert Alexander – bapt. 14 Oct 1822 (Baptism, **St. Mary, Pro Cathedral Parish (RC)**)

Margaret Unknown (mother):

Residence - Temple Street - October 14, 1822

- Unknown Alexander & Mary Maher

  o James Alexander – b. 1782, bapt. 1782 (Baptism, **St. Andrew Parish (RC)**)

- Unknown Alexander & Unknown

  o Mary Jane Alexander & John Atkinson – 1842 (Marriage, **St. Catherine Parish**)

Mary Jane Alexander (daughter):

Residence - Thomas Street - 1842

John Atkinson (son-in-law):

Occupation - Revenue Officer of Athlone - 1842

- Unknown Alexander & Unknown

    o David Alexander

Signature:

- Unknown Alexander & Unknown

    o David Alexander

Signature:

- Unknown Alexander & Unknown

    o George Alexander

Signature:

- Unknown Alexander & Unknown

    o George Alexander

Signature:

- Unknown Alexander & Unknown

  o George Alexander

Signature:

- Unknown Alexander & Unknown

  o Hannah Alexander

Signature:

- Unknown Alexander & Unknown

  o Henry Alexander

Signature:

- Unknown Alexander & Unknown

  o James Alexander

Signature:

- Unknown Alexander & Unknown

  o Jane Alexander

Signatures:

- Unknown Alexander & Unknown

  o John Alexander

Signature:

- Unknown Alexander & Unknown

  o John Alexander

Signature:

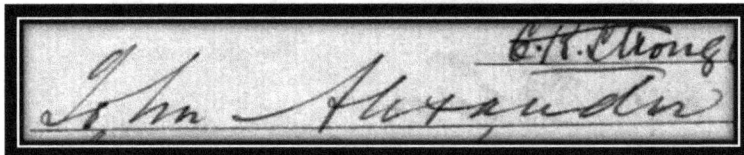

Alexander Surname Ireland: 1600s to 1900s

- Unknown Alexander & Unknown

  o Joseph Alexander

Signature:

- Unknown Alexander & Unknown

  o Marjorie Alexander

Signature:

- Unknown Alexander & Unknown

  o Matthew Alexander

Signature:

- Unknown Alexander & Unknown

  o Thomas Alexander

Signature:

Hurst

- Unknown Alexander & Unknown

  o Thomas Alexander

Signatures:

- William Alexander & Agnes Alexander

  o John Alexander – bapt. 11 May 1766 (Baptism, **St. Mary Parish**)

  o Mathias Alexander – bapt. 31 Jul 1768 (Baptism, **St. Mary Parish**)

William Alexander (father):

Residence - Mary's Abby - May 11, 1766

Boot Lune - July 31, 1768

- William Alexander & Anne Alexander

  o Elizabeth Alexander – bapt. 23 Nov 1741 (Baptism, **St. Catherine Parish**)

- William Alexander & Anne Alexander

  o Mary Alexander Alexander – bapt. 18 Sep 1763 (Baptism, **St. Mary Parish**)

- William Alexander & Anne Unknown

  o John Alexander – bapt. 26 Jan 1781 (Baptism, **St. Michan Parish (RC)**)

Alexander Surname Ireland: 1600s to 1900s

- William Alexander, bur. 11 Mar 1765 (Burial, **St. Luke Parish**) & Catherine Garrett, bur. 30 Oct 1755 (Burial, **St. Luke Parish**) – Apr 1718 (Marriage, **St. Luke Parish**)

  o Isabel Alexander – bapt. 7 Feb 1723 (Baptism, **St. Luke Parish**)

  o Mary Alexander – bur. 26 Jun 1731 (Burial, **St. Luke Parish**)

William Alexander (father):

Residence - Poddle - February 7, 1723

Occupation - Cordwinder - February 7, 1723

- William Alexander & Georgina Lear – 6 Jan 1829 (Marriage, **George Parish**)

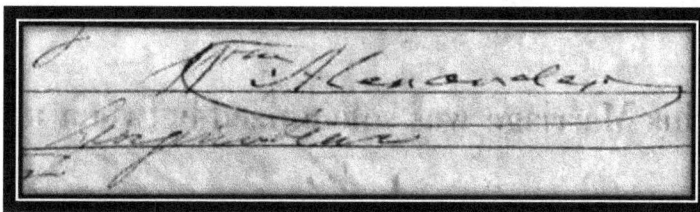

Signatures:

William Alexander (husband):

Residence - Richmond Place, St. George Parish - January 6, 1829

Occupation - Esquire - January 6, 1829

Georgina Lear (wife):

Residence - St. Thomas Parish, Dublin - January 6, 1829

Hurst

Wedding Witnesses:

Mary Burton & James Edmiston

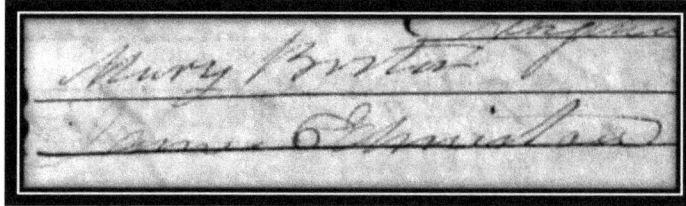

Signatures:

- William Alexander & Jessie Alexander
  - John Aleck Alexander – b. 22 Jan 1864, bapt. 3 Apr 1864 (Baptism, **St. Werburgh Parish**)

William Alexander (father):

Residence - **22 Castle Street - April 3, 1864**

Occupation - **Watchmaker - April 3, 1864**

- William Alexander & Margaret Munro – 25 Sep 1786 (Marriage, **St. Catherine Parish (RC)**)
- William Alexander & Mary Alexander
  - Samuel Alexander – bapt. 29 Nov 1795 (Baptism, **St. Luke Parish**)
- William Alexander & Mary Byrne (B y r n e)
  - Catherine Alexander – b. 1871, bapt. 1871 (Baptism, **St. Mary Parish (RC)**)
  - Anne Jane Alexander – b. 1872, bapt. 1872 (Baptism, **St. Mary Parish (RC)**)
  - Mary Agnes Alexander – b. 1875, bapt. 1875 (Baptism, **St. Mary Parish (RC)**)
  - John Joseph Alexander – b. 1876, bapt. 1876 (Baptism, **St. Mary Parish (RC)**)
- William Alexander & Mary Hemmings – 7 Dec 1758 (Marriage, **St. Paul Parish**)
- William Alexander & Mary Porter – 24 Nov 1736 (Marriage, **St. Mary Parish**)

Alexander Surname Ireland: 1600s to 1900s

- William Alexander & Mary Unknown

  o Anne Alexander – bapt. 14 May 1786 (Baptism, **St. Audoen Parish**)

- William Alexander & Mary Unknown

  o Sophie Alexander – bapt. 17 Jun 1817 (Baptism, **St. Mary, Pro Cathedral Parish** (RC))

- William Alexander & Mary Anne McCory – 6 Jan 1857 (Marriage, **St. Andrew Parish** (RC))

- William Alexander & Rose Alexander

  o Edward Alexander – bapt. 23 Jun 1834 (Baptism, **St. Mary, Pro Cathedral Parish** (RC))

- William Alexander & Unknown

  o William Alexander & Dorcas Adelaide Fennessy – 28 Jul 1847 (Marriage, **St. George Parish**)

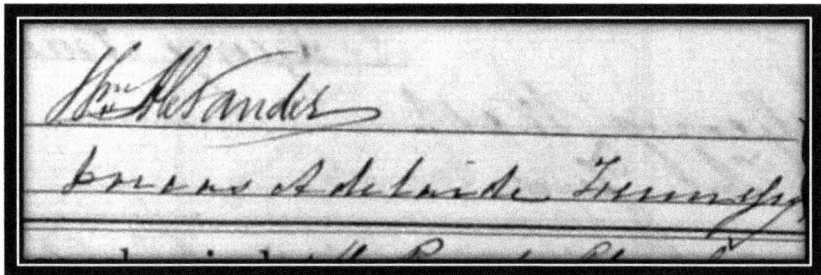

Signatures:

William Alexander (son):

Residence - Liverpool, Cloughton Parish, Birkenhead - July 28, 1847

Occupation - Merchant - July 28, 1847

Dorcas Adelaide Fennessy, daughter of Hugh Fennessy (daughter-in-law):

Residence - 7 Russell Place - July 28, 1847

Relationship Status at Marriage - minor

Hugh Fennessy (father):

Signature:

    Occupation - Gentleman

William Alexander (father):

    Occupation - Merchant

Wedding Witnesses:

Hugh Fennessy & Thomas Fennessy

Signatures:

- William Alexander & Unknown
  - Jane Alexander & William Rodgers – 12 Nov 1850 (Marriage, **St. Paul Parish**)

Signatures:

Alexander Surname Ireland: 1600s to 1900s

Jane Alexander (daughter):

    Residence - Temple Street - November 12, 1850

    Relationship Status at Marriage - minor age

William Rodgers, son of Richard Rodgers (son-in-law):

    Residence - Royal Barracks - November 12, 1850

    Occupation - Farrier, 12th Lancers - November 12, 1850

Richard Rodgers (father):

    Occupation - Boot & Shoe Maker

William Alexander (father):

    Occupation - Soldier, 12th Lancers

Wedding Witnesses:

George Basdell & Charlotte Fergus

Signatures:

Hurst

- William James Alexander & Gertrude Isabel Leticia Temple

  - Robert Quinn Alexander – bapt. 6 Jun 1816 (Baptism, **Taney Parish**)

Signature:

  - Mary Alexander – b. 13 Dec 1818, bapt. 9 Jan 1819 (Baptism, **St. Peter Parish**)

- William John Alexander & Isabel Alexander – 1 Mar 1815 (Marriage, **St. Peter Parish**)

William John Alexander (husband):

Residence - Swords - March 1, 1815

Isabel Alexander (wife):

Residence - St. Peter Parish - March 1, 1815

Wedding Witnesses:

Robert Alexander & William Alexander

Alexander Surname Ireland: 1600s to 1900s

Individual Births/Baptisms

- Catherine Staples Alexander – bapt. 30 May 1844 (Baptism, **Clontarf Parish**)

- George Alexander – bapt. 6 Oct 1864 (Baptism, **South Dublin Union Parish**)

- Margaret Alexander – bapt. 25 Jan 1746 (Baptism, **St. Paul Parish**)

- Thomas Alexander – bapt. 22 Dec 1678 (Baptism, **St. John Parish**)

Individual Burials

- Aaron Alexander – bur. 1 Jan 1813 (Burial, **St. Paul Parish**)

- Alice Moira Alexander – b. 1856, d. 19 Nov 1903, bur. 19 Nov 1903 (Burial, **Kilcrohane Parish**)

Alice Moira Alexander (deceased):

    Residence - Drimina, Sneem - November 19, 1903

    Age at Death - 47 years

- Anne Alexander – bur. 24 Dec 1777 (Burial, **St. Paul Parish**)

- Anne Alexander – bur. 10 Mar 1796 (Burial, **St. Peter Parish**)

Anne Alexander (deceased):

    Residence - Diggs Street - before March 10, 1796

- Anne Alexander – b. 1815, bur. 3 Nov 1821 (Burial, **St. Peter Parish**)

Anne Alexander (deceased):

    Residence - Liberty Lane - before November 3, 1821

    Age at Death - 6 years

    Place of Burial - St. Kevin's Church Yard

Hurst

- Anne Alexander – b. 1788, bur. 11 Jul 1849 (Burial, **St. Matthew Parish**)

Anne Alexander (deceased):

    Residence - Ring's End - before July 11, 1849

    Age at Death - 61 years

- Carroll Alexander – bur. 18 Aug 1780 (Burial, **St. Peter Parish**)

Carroll Alexander (deceased):

    Residence - Kevin Street - before August 18, 1780

- Elizabeth Alexander – bur. 30 Sep 1714 (Burial, **St. Audoen Parish**)

- Elizabeth Alexander – bur. 20 Sep 1751 (Burial, **St. Paul Parish**)

- Ellen Alexander – b. 1847, bur. 22 Jun 1850 (Burial, **St. Matthew Parish**)

Ellen Alexander (deceased):

    Residence - Ring's End - before June 22, 1850

    Age at Death - 3 years

- Francis Alexander – bur. 23 Jul 1629 (Burial, **St. John Parish**)

- George Alexander – b. 1854, bur. 16 Aug 1859 (Burial, **Irishtown Parish**)

George Alexander (deceased):

    Residence - Ring's End - before August 16, 1859

    Age at Death - 5 years

Alexander Surname Ireland: 1600s to 1900s

- George Alexander – b. 1864, d. 11 Nov 1865, bur. 1865 (Burial, **St. James Parish**)

George Alexander (deceased):

    Residence - South Dublin Union - November 11, 1865

    Age at Death - 1 year

- Hannah Alexander – bur. 24 Jul 1696 (Burial, **St. Peter Parish**)

Hannah Alexander (deceased):

    Residence - Lazer's Hill - before July 24, 1696

- Hierem Alexander – bur. Mar 1680 (Burial, **St. Peter Parish**)
- Honor Alexander – bur. 10 Apr 1827 (Burial, **St. Mary Parish**)

Honor Alexander (deceased):

    Residence - Capel Street - before April 10, 1827

- Hugh Alexander – bur. 1 Sep 1812 (Burial, **St. Mark Parish**)

Hugh Alexander (deceased):

    Residence - Liffey Street - September 1, 1812

- Ivy Alexander – b. Dec 1880, bur. 26 Mar 1881 (Burial, **George Parish**)

Ivy Alexander (deceased):

    Residence - 1 Jones Road - before March 26, 1881

    Age at Death - 4 months

Hurst

- James Alexander – bur. 16 Jun 1719 (Burial, **St. Peter Parish**)

- James Alexander – bur. 20 Jan 1808 (Burial, **St. Peter Parish**)

James Alexander (deceased):

   Residence - Dublin Nursery - before January 20, 1808

- James Alexander – b. 1725, bur. 14 Nov 1824 (Burial, **Clontarf Parish**)

James Alexander (deceased):

   Residence - Irishtown, Donnybrook Parish - before November 14, 1824

   Age at Death - 99 years

- James William Alexander – b. 1806, bur. 8 Nov 1826 (Burial, **St. Mary Parish**)

James William Alexander (deceased):

   Residence - Middle Mountjoy Street - before November 8, 1826

   Age at Death - 20 years

- Jane Alexander – bur. 31 Dec 1819 (Burial, **St. James Parish**)

Jane Alexander (deceased):

   Residence - Phibsboro - before December 31, 1819

- Jerome Alexander – d. 25 Jul 1670, bur. 28 Jul 1670 (Burial, **St. Patrick Parish**)

Jerome Alexander (deceased):

   Title - Sir

Alexander Surname Ireland: 1600s to 1900s

- John Alexander – bur. 2 Jan 1671 (Burial, **St. John Parish**)

John Alexander (deceased):

Occupation - Shoemaker - before January 2, 1671

- John Alexander – bur. 11 Jul 1736 (Burial, **St. Mark Parish**)

- John Alexander – b. 1823, bur. 12 May 1825 (Burial, **St. Peter Parish**)

John Alexander (deceased):

Residence - Cottage Terrace - before May 12, 1825

Age at Death - 2 years

- John Alexander – b. 1807, bur. 18 Mar 1840 (Burial, **St. Peter Parish**)

John Alexander (deceased):

Residence - Stephen Street - before March 18, 1840

Age at Death - 33 years

- John Alexander – b. 1849, bur. 27 May 1857 (Burial, **Irishtown Parish**)

John Alexander (deceased):

Residence - Ring's End - before May 27, 1857

Age at Death - 8 years

Hurst

- John Alexander – b. 27 Aug 1857, bur. 30 Aug 1857 (Burial, **Irishtown Parish**)

John Alexander (deceased):

    Residence - Ring's End - before August 30, 1857

    Age at Death - 3 days

- John Alexander – b. 1858, bur. 1 Jul 1863 (Burial, **Clontarf Parish**)

John Alexander (deceased):

    Residence - Haydon - before July 1, 1863

    Age at Death - 5 years

- John Alexander – b. 1815, bur. 4 Jan 1894 (Burial, **George Parish**)

John Alexander (deceased):

    Residence - 15 Longford Street - before January 4, 1894

    Age at Death - 79 years

- Jon Alexander – bur. 25 Jan 1727 (Burial, **St. Paul Parish**)

- Jonathan Alexander – bur. 20 Aug 1818 (Burial, **St. James Parish**)

Jonathan Alexander (deceased):

    Residence - James Street - before August 20, 1818

    Age at Death - child

- Joseph Alexander – bur. 3 Feb 1719 (Burial, **St. Peter Parish**)

- Joseph Alexander – bur. 7 Oct 1725 (Burial, **St. Paul Parish**)

Alexander Surname Ireland: 1600s to 1900s

- Luke Alexander – b. 1815, bur. 2 Jan 1855 (Burial, **Carlow Parish**)

Luke Alexander (deceased):

    Residence - Carlow - before January 2, 1855

    Age at Death - 40 years

- Margaret Alexander – bur. 19 Jul 1820 (Burial, **St. James Parish**)

Margaret Alexander (deceased):

    Residence - Phibsboro - before July 19, 1820

- Margaret Alexander – b. 1789, bur. 9 Mar 1816 (Burial, **St. Catherine Parish**)

Margaret Alexander (deceased):

    Residence - Thomas Street - before March 9, 1816

    Age at Death - 27 years

- Margaret Alexander – b. 1789, bur. 5 May 1848 (Burial, **St. Audoen Parish**)

Margaret Alexander (deceased):

    Residence - Hammond Lane - before May 5, 1848

    Age at Death - 59 years

- Mary Alexander – bur. 27 Aug 1814 (Burial, **St. Mary Parish**)

Mary Alexander (deceased):

    Residence - Britain Street - before August 27, 1814

- Mary Alexander – bur. 26 Sep 1720 (Burial, **St. Peter Parish**)

Mary Alexander (deceased):

> **Residence - Fleet Street - before September 26, 1720**

- Mary Alexander – d. 21 Jan 1829, bur. 1829 (Burial, **St. James Parish**)

Mary Alexander (deceased):

> **Residence - James Street - January 21, 1829**

- Mary Alexander – bur. 1830 (Burial, **St. James Parish**)

Mary Alexander (deceased):

> **Residence - James Street - before 1830**

- Mary Anne Alexander – bur. 29 Jul 1816 (Burial, **St. Paul Parish**)

- Matthew Alexander – bur. 9 Jun 1773 (Burial, **St. Peter Parish**)

- Matthew Alexander – b. 1755, bur. 7 Feb 1821 (Burial, **St. Peter Parish**)

Matthew Alexander (deceased):

> **Residence - Green Street - before February 7, 1821**

> **Age at Death - 66 years**

> **Place of Burial - St. Peter's Church Yard**

- Richard Alexander – bur. 8 Jul 1727 (Burial, **St. Paul Parish**)

- Robert Alexander – bur. 7 Mar 1730 (Burial, **St. Paul Parish**)

Alexander Surname Ireland: 1600s to 1900s

- Robert Alexander – bur. 15 May 1820 (Burial, **St. James Parish**)

Robert Alexander (deceased):

   Residence - Phibsboro - before May 15, 1820

- Rose Alexander – bur. 5 Aug 1704 (Burial, **St. Nicholas Without Parish**)

Rose Alexander (deceased):

   Residence - Mark's Alley - before August 5, 1704

- Samuel Alexander – bur. 20 Apr 1767 (Burial, **St. Luke Parish**)

Samuel Alexander (deceased):

   Residence - New Market - before April 20, 1767

   Cause of Death - decay

- Sarah Alexander – bur. 1 Mar 1814 (Burial, **St. Paul Parish**)

- Sarah Alexander – b. 1792, bur. 5 Dec 1819 (Burial, **St. Werburgh Parish**)

Sarah Alexander (deceased):

   Age at Death - 27 years

- St. George Alexander – bur. 9 Mar 1819 (Burial, **St. James Parish**)

St. George Alexander (deceased):

   Residence - James Street - before March 9, 1819

Hurst

- Thomas Alexander – bur. 2 May 1743 (Burial, **St. Paul Parish**)

Thomas Alexander (deceased):

    Age at Death - child

- Unknown Alexander – bur. 27 Dec 1679 (Burial, **St. Peter Parish**)

Unknown Alexander (deceased):

    Residence - St. Bride Parish - before December 27, 1679

- Unknown Alexander – bur. 9 May 1683 (Burial, **St. Peter Parish**)

Unknown Alexander (deceased):

    Residence - Sheep Street - before May 9, 1683

- Unknown Alexander – bur. 18 Sep 1738 (Burial, **St. Nicholas Without Parish**)

Unknown Alexander (deceased):

    Residence - St. Catherine Parish - before September 18, 1738

- Unknown Alexander – bur. 23 Jul 1786 (Burial, **St. John Parish**)

- Unknown Alexander – bur. 28 Jul 1786 (Burial, **St. John Parish**)

- Unknown Alexander – bur. 27 Aug 1796 (Burial, **St. John Parish**)

- Unknown Alexander (Mr.) – bur. 14 Jan 1819 (Burial, **St. Mary Parish**)

Unknown Alexander (Mr.) (deceased):

    Residence - Sheriff's Prison - before January 14, 1819

Alexander Surname Ireland: 1600s to 1900s

- Unknown Alexander (Mr.) – b. 1810, bur. 21 Jul 1831 (Burial, **St. Mary Parish**)

Unknown Alexander (Mr.) (deceased):

  Residence - Sackville Street - before July 21, 1831

  Age at Death - 21 years

- Unknown Alexander (Mrs.) – bur. 10 Sep 1779 (Burial, **St. Nicholas Without Parish**)

Unknown Alexander (Mrs.) (deceased):

  Residence - Coombe - before September 10, 1779

- W. Alexander – bur. 3 Nov 1743 (Burial, **St. Nicholas Without Parish**)

W. Alexander (deceased):

  Residence - Weaver's EQ - before November 3, 1743

- William Alexander – bur. 4 Mar 1700 (Burial, **St. Peter Parish**)

William Alexander (deceased):

  Residence - Lazer's Hill - before March 4, 1700

- William Alexander – bur. 2 Jun 1721 (Burial, **St. Nicholas Without Parish**)

William Alexander (deceased):

  Residence - Patrick Street - June 2, 1721

- William Alexander – bur. 6 Nov 1734 (Burial, **St. Peter Parish**)

Hurst

- William Alexander – bur. 13 Jan 1738 (Burial, **St. Mary Parish**)

William Alexander (deceased):

   Social Status - a poor man

- William Alexander – bur. 16 May 1767 (Burial, **St. Paul Parish**)

William Alexander (deceased):

   Residence - High Street - before May 16, 1767

   Occupation - Gentleman - May 16, 1767

- William Alexander – bur. 27 Feb 1820 (Burial, **St. James Parish**)

William Alexander (deceased):

   Residence - Phibsboro - before February 27, 1820

- William Alexander – bur. 13 Jan 1821 (Burial, **St. Mark Parish**)
- William Alexander – b. Feb 1855, bur. 5 Mar 1856 (Burial, **Irishtown Parish**)

William Alexander (deceased):

   Residence - Ring's End - before March 5, 1856

   Age at Death - 11 months

Individual Marriages

- Adelaide Alexander & Terrance Colvin

  - George Colvin – bapt. 29 Aug 1837 (Baptism, **St. Michan Parish (RC)**)

- Anne Alexander & Edward Vincent Bolger

  - William Joseph Bolger – bapt. 1 Sep 1845 (Baptism, **St. Nicholas Parish (RC)**)

  - Henrietta Bolger – b. 1 Aug 1857, bapt. 4 Sep 1857 (Baptism, **St. Mary, Pro Cathedral Parish (RC)**)

Edward Bolger (father):

Residence - 10 Mecklenburgh Street - September 4, 1857

- Anne Alexander & Edward Nugent – 27 Apr 1868 (Marriage, **St. Mary Parish (RC)**)

  - Mary Anne Nugent – b. 1869, bapt. 1869 (Baptism, **St. Andrew Parish (RC)**)

  - Anne Jane Nugent – b. 1871, bapt. 1871 (Baptism, **St. Andrew Parish (RC)**)

  - Michael Nugent – b. 1875, bapt. 1875 (Baptism, **St. Andrew Parish (RC)**)

  - John Nugent – b. 1878, bapt. 1878 (Baptism, **St. Andrew Parish (RC)**)

  - Edward Nugent – b. 1880, bapt. 1880 (Baptism, **St. Andrew Parish (RC)**)

  - Christopher Nugent – b. 1882, bapt. 1882 (Baptism, **St. Andrew Parish (RC)**)

  - Cecelia Nugent – b. 1883, bapt. 1883 (Baptism, **St. Andrew Parish (RC)**)

  - William Wallace Nugent – b. 1886, bapt. 1886 (Baptism, **St. Andrew Parish (RC)**)

  - Cornelius (C o r n e l i u s) Francis Nugent – b. 1891, bapt. 1891 (Baptism, **St. Andrew Parish (RC)**)

  - Joseph Edward Nugent – b. 1892, bapt. 1892 (Baptism, **St. Andrew Parish (RC)**)

127

Hurst

Edward Nugent (father):

Residence - 79 Brunswick Street - 1871

1878

75 Great Brunswick Street - 1875

1882

1883

75 Brunswick Street - 1869

1880

79 Great Brunswick Place - 1886

32 Erne Street - 1891

6 Hamilton Row - 1892

- Anne Alexander & Joseph Corrigan
  - Catherine Corrigan – b. 25 Jun 1861, bapt. 28 Jun 1861 (Baptism, **St. Mary, Pro Cathedral Parish** (RC))

Joseph Corrigan (father):

Residence - Rotunda - June 28, 1861

- Anne Alexander & O'Hanlon John O'Neil
  - Joseph O'Neil – b. 15 May 1867, bapt. 27 May 1867 (Baptism, **SS. Michael & John Parish** (RC))

Alexander Surname Ireland: 1600s to 1900s

O'Hanlon John O'Neil (father):

Residence - 10 Castle Street - May 27, 1867

- Anne Alexander & Patrick Byrne (B y r n e)
  - Jane Byrne (B y r n e) – b. 16 Jan 1885, bapt. 19 Jan 1885 (Baptism, **St. Mary, Haddington** Road Parish (RC))

Patrick Byrne (father):

Residence - 81 Bath Avenue - January 19, 1885

- Anne Alexander & Richard Johnson – 6 Oct 1764 (Marriage, **St. Mary Parish**)

Richard Johnson (husband):

Occupation - Esquire - October 6, 1764

- Anne Mary Alexander & Gulielmo Redmond – 27 Dec 1807 (Marriage, **St. Andrew Parish** (RC))
- Catherine Alexander & Charles Christopher Nugent – 31 Jan 1864 (Marriage, **St. Mary Parish** (RC))
  - Michael Nugent – b. 1864, bapt. 1864 (Baptism, **St. Mary Parish** (RC))
  - Mary Nugent – b. 1866, bapt. 1866 (Baptism, **St. Mary Parish** (RC))
  - Catherine Nugent – b. 1868, bapt. 1868 (Baptism, **St. Mary Parish** (RC))
  - Sarah Anne Nugent – b. 1870, bapt. 1870 (Baptism, **St. Mary Parish** (RC))
  - Christine Nugent – b. 1872, bapt. 1872 (Baptism, **St. Mary Parish** (RC))
  - Christopher Nugent – b. 1875, bapt. 1875 (Baptism, **St. Mary Parish** (RC))

- Edward Christopher Nugent – b. 22 Jan 1877, bapt. 29 Jan 1877 (Baptism, **St. Mary, Pro Cathedral Parish** (RC))

- Christine Catherine Nugent – b. 29 May 1879, bapt. 30 May 1879 (Baptism, **St. Mary, Pro Cathedral Parish** (RC))

- Cornelius (C o r n e l i u s) Francis Nugent – b. 23 Jun 1881, bapt. 27 Jun 1881 (Baptism, **St. Mary, Pro Cathedral Parish** (RC))

- Gerald Alfred Nugent – b. 3 Sep 1883, bapt. 7 Sep 1883 (Baptism, **St. Mary, Pro Cathedral Parish** (RC))

- Albert Patrick Nugent – b. 17 Mar 1886, bapt. 19 Mar 1886 (Baptism, **St. Mary, Pro Cathedral Parish** (RC))

- Valentine George Nugent – b. 15 Feb 1888, bapt. 17 Feb 1888 (Baptism, **St. Mary, Pro Cathedral Parish** (RC))

Charles Christopher Nugent (father):

Residence - 41 Upper Buckingham Street - January 29, 1877

March 19, 1886

February 17, 1888

41 Buckingham Street - May 30, 1879

39 Upper Buckingham Street - June 27, 1881

39 Buckingham Street - September 7, 1883

Alexander Surname Ireland: 1600s to 1900s

- Catherine Alexander & Robert Hamilton – 12 Jun 1797 (Marriage, **St. Anne Parish**)

Robert Hamilton (husband):

  Occupation - Esquire - June 12, 1797

- Christian Alexander & Thomas Wilbram – 16 Jul 1683 (Marriage, **St. Audoen Parish**)
- Eleanor Alexander & George Connolly – Nov 1845 (Marriage, **St. Catherine Parish (RC)**)
  - Margaret Connolly – bapt. Oct 1846 (Baptism, **St. Catherine Parish (RC)**)
  - Michael Connolly & Thomasina Whyter – 13 Apr 1874 (Marriage, **Harrington Street Parish (RC)**)

Michael Connally (son):

  Residence - 7 St. Maurice Lane - April 13, 1874

Thomasina Whyter, daughter of Thomas Whyter & Elizabeth Kinsella

(daughter-in-law):

  Residence - West Malpas Street - April 13, 1874

  - Ellen Mary Connolly – b. 1861, bapt. 1861 (Baptism, **St. Andrew Parish (RC)**)
  - Robert Connolly – b. 1865, bapt. 1865 (Baptism, **St. Andrew Parish (RC)**)

George Connolly (father):

  Residence - 8 Trinity Place - 1861

  1865

Wedding Witnesses:

Elizabeth Steward & Joseph Alexander

Hurst

- Eleanor Alexander & Morney (M o r n e y) Coppin – 7 Feb 1839 (Marriage, **St. Werburgh Parish**)

Signatures:

Eleanor Alexander (wife):

> Residence - St. Werburgh Parish - February 7, 1839

Morney Coppin (husband):

> Residence - St. Andrew Parish - February 7, 1839

Wedding Witnesses:

Robert Stevelly & M. Owen

Signatures:

- Elizabeth Alexander & Charles Henry – 27 Jan 1804 (Marriage, **George Parish**)

Elizabeth Alexander (wife):

> Residence - St. George Parish - January 27, 1804

Charles Henry (husband):

> Residence - Mountjoy Square - January 27, 1804

Alexander Surname Ireland: 1600s to 1900s

Occupation - Servant - January 27, 1804

- Elizabeth Alexander & John Hamilton – 16 Jun 1797 (Marriage, **St. Anne Parish**)

John Hamilton (husband):

Occupation - Esquire - June 16, 1797

- Elizabeth Alexander & Thomas Grumley (G r u m l e y) – 30 Sep 1783 (Marriage, **St. Catherine Parish (RC)**)
  - Michael Grumley (G r u m l e y) – bapt. 26 Sep 1784 (Baptism, **St. Catherine Parish (RC)**)
- Emily Alexander & John Colthurst – 1 May 1824 (Marriage, **Carlow Parish**)
- Esther Alexander & Thomas Murphy – 12 Aug 1820 (Marriage, **Lucan Parish (RC)**) (Marriage, **St. Mary, Haddington Road Parish (RC)**)

Wedding Witnesses:

Margaret Alexander, Thomas Heffernan, & Jane Heffernan

- Frances Alexander & John Barry
  - Frances Barry – bapt. Jan 1816 (Baptism, **St. Nicholas Parish (RC)**)
  - Henry Barry – bapt. Jul 1818 (Baptism, **St. Nicholas Parish (RC)**)
- Hannah Dorothy Margaret Alexander & John McClaghen – 7 Dec 1705 (Marriage, **St. Michan Parish**)

John McClaghen (husband):

Occupation - Gentleman - December 7, 1705

Hurst

- Harriet Catherine Alexander & John Watson Wakefield – 26 Jun 1837 (Marriage, **George Parish**)

Signatures:

Harriet Catherine Alexander (wife):

    Residence - 45 Great George's Street, St. George Parish - June 26, 1837

        Portglenone House, Co. Antrim - June 26, 1837

John Watson Wakefield (husband):

    Residence - Brook Hill, Lisburn, St. Thomas Parish - June 26, 1837

        Gresham's Hotel, Sackville Street - June 26, 1837

Wedding Witnesses:

Nathaniel Meath, Thomas Staples, James Watson, & John Murphy

Signatures:

Alexander Surname Ireland: 1600s to 1900s

- Henrietta Frances Alexander & Robert Smyth – 19 May 1830 (Marriage, **George Parish**)

Signatures:

Henrietta Frances Alexander (wife):

Residence - St. George Parish - May 19, 1830

Robert Smyth (husband):

Residence - Gaybrook, Co. Westminster - May 19, 1830

Occupation - Esquire - May 19, 1830

Wedding Witnesses:

Nathaniel Meath, James Alexander, and Thomas Walsh

Signatures:

- Ida Alexander & John Reynard
  - Mary Josephine Reynard – b. 12 Mar 1880, bapt. 20 Apr 1880 (Baptism, **St. James Parish (RC)**)
  - Patrick Joseph Reynard – b. 12 Mar 1880, bapt. 20 Apr 1880 (Baptism, **St. James Parish (RC)**)

Hurst

John Reynard (father):

Residence - 37 James Street - April 20, 1880

- Isabel Alexander & James Orr (O r r)

  o Patrick Orr (O r r) – b. 18 Feb 1862, bapt. 19 Feb 1862 (Baptism, **St. Mary, Pro Cathedral Parish (RC)**)

James Orr (father):

Residence - 19 Gloucester Place - February 19, 1862

- Jane Alexander & Cosby Eaton – 11 Apr 1779 (Marriage, **St. John Parish**)

- Jane Alexander & George Smyth – 14 Jun 1847 (Marriage, **St. Nicholas Parish (RC)**)

- Jane Alexander & James Campbell – 17 Aug 1749 (Marriage, **St. Mark Parish**)

- Jane Alexander & Michael Smyth

  o Catherine Smyth – bapt. 4 Sep 1846 (Baptism, **St. Nicholas Parish (RC)**)

- Jane Alexander & William Williams – 6 Jan 1738 (Marriage, **St. Mark Parish**)

- Joan Alexander & William Proctor

  o Elizabeth Proctor – b. 20 Feb 1876, bapt. 12 Mar 1876 (Baptism, **Tralee Parish (RC)**)

William Proctor (father):

Residence - Ballymullen - March 12, 1876

- Lillian A. Alexander & William Smyth

  o Lillian May Smyth – b. 19 May 1911, bapt. 28 Jul 1911 (Baptism, **Tralee Parish**)

William Smyth (father):

Residence - Ballymullen, Tralee - July 28, 1911

Alexander Surname Ireland: 1600s to 1900s

Occupation - Manager, Leather Store - July 28, 1911

- Margaret Alexander & Cornelius (C o r n e l i u s) Brennan – 9 Jan 1843 (Marriage, **St. Nicholas Parish (RC)**)

- Margaret Alexander & Dominick McDermott (M c D e r m o t t)
  - Charles McDermott (M c D e r m o t t) – bapt. 5 Jul 1833 (Baptism, **St. Nicholas Parish (RC)**)

- Mary Alexander & George O'Neill
  - Anne O'Neill & John Cooke – 24 Feb 1879 (Marriage, **St. Nicholas Parish (RC)**)

Anne O'Neill (daughter):

Residence - 49 Golden Lane - February 24, 1879

John Cooke, son of William Cooke & Elizabeth Unknown (son-in-law):

Residence - 15 --, Naas - February 24, 1879

Wedding Witnesses:

Thomas Cooke & Catherine McDonnell

- Mary Alexander & James Michael Patrick Dunne
  - Martha Dunne – b. 4 Sep 1870, bapt. 12 Sep 1870 (Baptism, **SS. Michael & John Parish (RC)**)
  - Mary Christine Dunne – b. 17 Dec 1871, bapt. 28 Dec 1871 (Baptism, **SS. Michael & John Parish (RC)**)
  - Thomas Dunne – b. 23 Nov 1872, bapt. 28 Nov 1872 (Baptism, **SS. Michael & John Parish (RC)**)
  - Mary Margaret Dunne – b. 7 Jul 1875, bapt. 9 Jul 1875 (Baptism, **St. Audoen Parish (RC)**)

Hurst

- o Bridget Dunne – b. 13 Mar 1877, bapt. 20 Mar 1877 (Baptism, **St. Audoen Parish (RC)**)

- o Patrick Dunne – b. 26 Dec 1879, bapt. 30 Dec 1879 (Baptism, **St. Audoen Parish (RC)**)

- o Mary Dunne – b. 9 Sep 1881, bapt. 9 Sep 1881 (Baptism, **St. Audoen Parish (RC)**)

- o Esther Dunne – b. 17 Feb 1883, bapt. 20 Feb 1883 (Baptism, **St. Audoen Parish (RC)**)

James Dunne (father):

Residence - 19 Black Hall Row - September 12, 1870

Black Hall Row - December 28, 1871

4 Black Lane - November 28, 1872

22 Black Hall Row - July 9, 1875

12 Black Hall Row - March 20, 1877

21 Black Hall Row - December 30, 1879

35 Black Hall Row - September 9, 1881

25 Black Hall Row - February 20, 1883

- • Mary Alexander & John Brophy

  - o Daniel Brophy – b. 2 Nov 1812, bapt. 8 Nov 1812 (Baptism, **St. Catherine Parish (RC)**)

- • Mary Alexander & John Lord – 19 Nov 1774 (Marriage, **St. James Parish**)

John Lord (husband):

Occupation - Soldier - November 19, 1774

- • Mary Alexander & John Rowan

  - o Christopher Rowan – b. 25 Dec 1865, bapt. 28 Dec 1865 (Baptism, **SS. Michael & John Parish (RC)**)

- o Joseph Rowan – b. 20 Sep 1867, bapt. 23 Sep 1867 (Baptism, **SS. Michael & John Parish (RC)**)

John Rowan (father):

Residence - 28 Back Lane - December 28, 1865

22 upper Black Hall Row - September 23, 1867

- Mary A. Alexander & Michael Gibson
  - o Sarah Gibson – b. 13 Jan 1892, bapt. 15 Jan 1892 (Baptism, **Harrington Street Parish (RC)**)

Michael Gibson (father):

Residence - 68 Lower Clanbrassil Street - January 15, 1892

- Mary Anne Alexander & Michael Gorman (G o r m a n)
  - o Mary Anne Gorman (G o r m a n) – bapt. 29 Jan 1849 (Baptism, **St. Nicholas Parish (RC)**)
- Mary Anne Alexander & William Strong
  - o Mary Susan Strong – b. 28 Nov 1877, bapt. 8 Dec 1904 (Baptism, **Rathmines Parish (RC)**)

William Strong (father):

Residence - 4 Dartmouth Road - December 8, 1904

- Mary Ellen Alexander & Edmund Hubert
  - o Eleanor Emma Hubert – b. 8 Mar 1899, bapt. 8 Mar 1899 (Baptism, **Rathmines Parish (RC)**)

Hurst

Edmund Hubert (father):

Residence - 4 Harold's Cross Cottages - March 8, 1899

- Mary Jane Alexander & Luke Kelly – 2 Jun 1840 (Marriage, **St. Andrew Parish (RC)**)

    o   Peter Kelly – bapt. 4 Aug 1848 (Baptism, **St. Catherine Parish (RC)**)

    o   Emily Kelly – bapt. 1 May 1851 (Baptism, **St. Catherine Parish (RC)**)

    o   Alexander Francis Kelly, bapt. 4 Mar 1856 (Baptism, **St. Catherine Parish (RC)**) & Margaret Gannon – 1 Aug 1892 (Marriage, **Rathmines Parish (RC)**)

Alexander Francis Kelly (son):

Residence - 127 Francis Street - August 1, 1892

Margaret Gannon, daughter of William Gannon & Catherine Evans

(daughter-in-law):

Residence - 27 Lower Mount Pleasant Avenue - August 1, 1892

    o   Agnes Clare Kelly – b. 22 Apr 1858, bapt. 30 Apr 1858 (Baptism, **St. Catherine Parish (RC)**)

    o   Lucy Kelly – b. 31 Jul 1860, bapt. 3 Aug 1860 (Baptism, **St. Catherine Parish (RC)**)

Luke Kelly (father):

Residence - 132 Cork Street - April 30, 1858

103 Cork Street - August 3, 1860

Alexander Surname Ireland: 1600s to 1900s

- Mary Margaret Alexander & Richard Lynam

  o Mary Lynam – bapt. 20 Jul 1768 (Baptism, **St. James Parish** (RC))

  o Anne Lynam – bapt. 2 Aug 1773 (Baptism, **St. James Parish** (RC))

  o James Lynam – bapt. 21 Aug 1779 (Baptism, **St. Catherine Parish** (RC))

  o Joseph Lynam – bapt. 21 Aug 1779 (Baptism, **St. Catherine Parish** (RC))

- Phebe Alexander & John Weller – Apr 1750 (Marriage, **St. Catherine Parish** (RC))

- Sarah Alexander & William Henry Lattimore

  o Henry Lattimore – b. 1876, bapt. 10 Jan 1876 (Baptism, **St. James Parish** (RC))

William Henry Lattimore (father):

Residence - No. 9 Irwin Street - January 10, 1876

- Sarah Teresa Alexander & James Walker – 19 Jun 1823 (Marriage, **St. Mary, Pro Cathedral Parish** (RC))

- Susan Alexander & James Agar – 10 Jan 1692 (Marriage, **St. Michan Parish**)

Susan Alexander (wife):

Residence - St. Michan Parish, Co. Dublin - January 10, 1692

James Agar (husband):

Residence - Gowran, Co. Killkeany - January 10, 1692

Occupation - Gentleman - January 10, 1692

Name Variations

Includes Latin and Abbreviated forms of names found in the original documents.

Abigail = Abigale, Abigall

Anne = Ann, Anna, Annae

Bartholomew = Barth, Bartholmeus, Bartholomeo

Bridget = Birgis, Brigid, Brigida, Bridgit

Catherine = Catharine, Catharina, Catharinae, Catherina, Cath, Catha, Cathae, Cathe, Cathn

Charles = Carolus, Charls, Chas

Christopher = Christoph

Daniel = Danielem, Danielis

Edmund = Edmond

Edward = Ed, Edwd

Eleanor = Eleo, Eleonora, Elinor, Ellenor

Elizabeth = Betty, Elisa, Elisabeth, Eliz, Eliza, Elizab, Elizh, Elizth

Ellen = Elena, Ellena

Emily = Emilia

Esther = Essie, Ester

Frances = Fannie, Fanny

Francis = Fransicum

George = Geo, Georg, Georgius

Grace = Gratiae

Gulielmo = Guil, Guillelmi, Gulielmum, Guillelmus, Gulmi

Alexander Surname Ireland: 1600s to 1900s

Harold = Harry

Helen = Helena

Honor = Hanora, Honora

James = Jacobi, Jacobus, Jas

Jane = Joanna

Jeanne = Jeannae, Joannae

Joan = Johanna, Joney

John = Jno, Joannem, Joannes, Johannis

Joseph = Jos

Juliana = Julian

Leticia = Letitia, Lettice, Letticia

Margaret = Margarita, Margaritae, Margeret, Marget, Margt

Mary = Maria, My

Mary Anne = Marianna, Marianne, Maryanne

Michael = Michaelis, Michl

Patrick = Pat, Patt, Patk, Patricii, Patricius

Peter = Petri

Richard = Ricardi, Ricardus, Rich, Richd

Robert = Roberti

Rose = Rosa, Rosae

Samuel = Samuelis

Thomas = Thom, Thomae, Thoms, Thos, Ths

Timothy = Timotheus, Timy

William = Wil, Will, Willm, Wm

Notes

Notes

Notes

Notes

Notes

Notes

Index

Hurst

Alexander Surname Ireland: 1600s to 1900s

Births

Hurst

Alexander Surname Ireland: 1600s to 1900s

Hurst

B

D

Alexander Surname Ireland: 1600s to 1900s

R

S

T

U

V

W

Hurst

About The Author

Donovan Hurst graduated from San Diego State University with a Bachelor of Arts in the major field of studies of History and a minor in the field of studies of Anthropology. He is a current member of The General Society of Mayflower Descendants and has been conducting genealogical research for over 10 years tracing back his ancestors to their ancestral homelands in Denmark, England, France, Germany, Ireland, Norway, and Scotland.

www.ingramcontent.com/pod-product-compliance
Lightning Source LLC
Chambersburg PA
CBHW081151270326
41930CB00014B/3114